THE **GUARDIAN** BOOK OF

SPORTS

Quotes

THE **GUARDIAN** BOOK OF

SPORTS

Quotes

Edited by John Samuel

Macdonald
Queen Anne Press

A *Queen Anne Press* BOOK

© John Samuel 1985

First published in 1985 by
Queen Anne Press, a division of
Macdonald & Co (Publishers) Ltd,
Maxwell House, 74 Worship Street,
London EC2A 2EN

A BPCC plc Company

Cartoons: Les Gibbard
Design: Clare Forte

British Library Cataloguing in Publication Data

The Guardian book of sports quotes.
  1. Sports—Anecdotes, facetiae, satire, etc.
  I. Samuel, John
  796'.0207   GV707

  ISBN 0-356-10730-2

Typeset by Acorn Bookwork,
Salisbury, Wiltshire

Printed and bound in Great Britain by
Hazell Watson & Viney Ltd,
Member of the BPCC Group, Aylesbury, Bucks.

CONTENTS

FOREWORD

Newspaper writers and editors ought to have in common a skill and enjoyment in precis—the verbal reduction of an event or happening to its quintessential. The quote (still guarded with 'n.colloq.' in the *Oxford Dictionary*) is a joyful playmate of the same craft. A quotation is not quite the same thing. It is certainly a 'borrowed' passage of speech or writing, but its roots are in an age without television or the jet engine. Alas, some will say—but modern life is as it is. The quote is an Americanism which has transplanted well because Britons these days less readily make a point by evading it. Sociologists can muse on the reasons for this. The quote of today may command wit, wisdom or humour. Essentially it must be brief, its point made with a minimum of preamble or explanation. It may be oblique, often it will carry nuance.

We began Sports Quotes of the Year as a Christmas entertainment in 1971. Frank Keating, then as now a writer of warmth and humour, with the help of colleagues collated them for eleven years, since when Phil Shaw primarily has been responsible, and indeed has presented his own diverting book of Soccer quotes. The *Guardian Book of Sports Quotes* reflects our interests and humours across a span of years and a spread of sports. They have been chosen not necessarily because they have appeared in the *Guardian* but because they say something which ought not to be discarded, unlike most newspaper material written only for the day. I have restored some quotes which had to be cut for space purposes, and arbitrarily included others not to hand at the time.

As one puts them together, a tapestry of sporting history emerges. Some of the patterns are linked, others of the moment. Fourteen years represents less than one generation of golfers or cricketers, two or three of swimmers. Names paddle back. In our first ever Quotes, Don Schollander, the champion US swimmer, was saying, 'When I retired I was

22. A swimmer does not get punched or clobbered, no cuts, bruises or broken bones, and I was an amateur not a professional; but I had had it. I was tired and I had been tired for three years.' In the next column there was Geoffrey Boycott saying, 'I am still badly feeling the effect of my injury and will not be returning to the Yorkshire side for some time'. This after scoring 138 in a club match.

In November 1984 Sid Fielden, a pro-Boycott man the previous winter, said of the Yorkshire cricketer's dual role as a player and committee man, 'I would like him to resign but I don't think there's an earthly chance of his doing so'. Ironic, too, in 1984, a year of Yorkshire cricketing and mining strife, to turn back to 1975 and find Ray Illingworth, a man in and out of Yorkshire affairs, saying, 'This mining strike is ridiculous. There's tea ladies at the top of a mine who are earning more than county cricketers. Arthur Scargill ought to come down here and try bowling 20 overs.'

It was a tricky problem whether to collate the quotes year by year or sport by sport. In the end it was the latter, in chronological order, because that seemed to provide an important extra dimension. Neville Cardus, one of the greatest of *Guardian* sports writers, once said, 'Judge every man against the context of his time'. As a moral imperative that is unassailable, but there are curious shades and lights when attitudes at a certain point are contrasted with known fate. George Best's 'I go, I come back...' in 1973 touches a raw nerve. Jimmy Connors' 'Mister bastard to you' the following year, talks back to a Wimbledon heckler with a vein of humour absent in his 1984 exchanges with the Davis Cup umpire in Stockholm.

Whether sport is serious or frivolous, important or unimportant, I leave to those who like to distinguish between hitting a good, clean four iron, scoring a goal off the knee cap, or paying the gas bill. These quotes do not seek to distinguish. Everyone will have his or her favourites. I like the sardonic humour of Bep Guidolin, coach of the Kansas City Scouts, 'I don't have nightmares about my team. You gotta sleep before you have nightmares.' Or, a misprint of which the *Guardian* would have been proud, in a Jamaica newspaper, 'E.W. Swanton—Sort of a Cricket Peron'. Or Ernie Tagg, Crewe manager, on Stan Bowles in 1974, 'If he could pass a betting shop like he can pass a ball we'd have no worries at all'. After-dinner speakers are invited to borrow as they will. We do not pretend these quotes are exclusive, and apologise in advance for any well-remembered lines we have overlooked or did not scoop up. Apologies to fellow media people caught out in all too familiar howlers under the peculiar pressures of sports events. We've a few of our own. To all, please enjoy.

66 He just can't believe what's not happening to him. **99**

DAVID COLEMAN

1973

My back is ruined so I can't sit still for long. The game has given me arthritis in my neck from butting people with my head, and if I walk too much my knees swell.—**Peter Gent,** 31, retiring US footballer.

1975

I don't have nightmares about my team. You gotta sleep before you have nightmares.—**Bep Guidolin,** coach to Kansas City Scouts.

1976

Class in a football coach is, when they finally run you out of town, to look like you're leading the parade.—**Bill Battle,** sacked Tennessee manager.

I won't mention the name of this particular team we were playing, but at half time we came in, pulled off our socks and began putting iodine on the teeth marks in our legs.—**Red Grange,** remembering a particularly strenuous afternoon of college football.

1977

A leading American football player was asked on television whether he preferred Astroturf or grass. He replied, 'I don't know, man, I've never smoked Astroturf.'—**Tim Fell**.

1978

I resigned as coach because of illness and fatigue. The fans were sick and tired of me.—**John Ralston**, Denver Broncos.

1980

In this game all you need is speed, strength and an ability to recognise pain immediately.—**Reggie Williams**, Cincinnati linebacker.

1981

I myself would like to see more white athletes. I think they are overlooking a good profession. I don't think it is good for the league to have all-black teams and 95 per cent white audiences.—Cleveland Cavaliers owner **Ted Stepien**.

1982

Cocaine arrived in my life with my first-round draft into the NFL in 1974. It has dominated my life. . . . Eventually, it took control and almost killed me. . . . Cocaine may be found in quantity throughout the NFL. It's pushed on players. ... Sometimes it's pushed *by* players. ... Just as it controlled me, it now controls and corrupts the game, because so many players are on it.—**Don Reese**, in a special article written for *Sports Illustrated*.

1983

I'm sure the British public will wonder why the players have so much protective equipment. What they'll be watching is disciplined violence. At ground level you can hear the impact. When two 250 lb players run into each other, it's like ammunition.—**Pete Rozelle**, NFL commissioner, on American football at Wembley.

I wouldn't want to play rugby. That's a very dangerous game.—**St Louis Cardinals player** at Wembley in August.

1971

We're treated like schoolchildren by the Board. Run here,
don't run there, is all we get. We're amateur sportsmen.
Why can't we decide our own lives?—**Dick Taylor**.

About 50 metres out from the finish I began to think I've
won, that's it. I had a feeling of contentment, almost
complacency. And that's when, unforgiveably, I lost my
concentration. They all came up on me and with a shock I
thought, blast, I've lost. Then I thought, never mind, I'm
only 19.—**David Jenkins**, after winning the European 400
metres in Helsinki.

I am still looking for shoes that will make running on
streets seem like running barefoot across the bosoms of
maidens.—**Dave Bronson**, US marathon runner.

We were all running for Lilian.—**Vera Nicholi**, 800 metres winner in Helsinki.

1972
When I first got back to Belfast with my gold medal the soldiers had a geiger counter which went click, click, click. 'You've got a large piece of metal in there,' they said. But I ended up signing their flak jackets.—**Mary Peters**.

Sheila Sherwood told me that I blew so many kisses to the crowd after every jump that I could have got the job at the very end of the Morecombe and Wise Show.—**Mary Peters**.

1973
It is tragic that so much effort goes into athletics and yet the lack of inspired administration remains an insult to the aspirations of the young. Like others, I am going to emigrate wishing I could have helped the sport in my own country.—**Lynn Davies**.

The money, it's cool. Why shouldn't we be paid like everyone else in our society? I just don't understand the amateur ethic out of another century.—Pro high jumper **John Radetich**, after setting a world indoor record of 7 feet, 4¾ inches.

Dave Bedford amazes me: the gay bachelor with his car and his new job. The way he packs it all in: he'll run 14 miles at 7 a.m. and another 14 at 5 p.m. and then go out to eat and drink. I just couldn't do it. He can.—**Brendan Foster**.

I'm the last of the amateurs—and considering how I jump I reckon it's just as well.—**Mike Campbell**, British high-jump champion.

1974

There are only two alternatives to taking anabolic steroids—don't take them and be second class, or give up athletics.—**Howard Payne**.

Winning is simply concentration, application and confidence.—**Brendan Foster**.

1975

World records are like shirts. Anyone can have one if he works for it.—**Filbert Bayi**.

The bad facilities in Britain have created a monstrous hybrid, the neurotic pole vaulter. You have seen him, irritatingly hesitant at the end of the runway, pole nervously clenched and unclenched, fidgeting fingers being hysterically demanded elsewhere to adjust socks, shorts, and general dishevelment. Eros, the life instinct, is fighting back, arguing the case for survival in the face of folly.—**Mike Bull**.

Running for money doesn't make you run fast. It makes you run first.—**Ben Jipcho**.

When I was training I didn't care about nobody or nothing. And I even refused crumpet on Saturdays.—**Charles Clover**, former javelin thrower.

1976
Running a marathon is just like reading a good book. After a while you're just not conscious of the physical act of reading.—**Frank Shorter**.

My first 18 ft vault wasn't any more of a thrill than my first clearance of 15 ft or 16 ft or 17 ft. I just had more time to enjoy it on the way down.—**Roland Carter**, US pole-vaulter.

Frank Clement lost the 800 simply because he was never able to get into the right position.—**Ron Pickering**.

All society is based on specialists. Except the decathlon. The decathlon is a presentation of moderation.—**Bruce Jenner**, Olympic champion.

It's funny to me, why they make Montreal marathon downhill all the way.—**Waldemar Cierpinski**, Olympic marathon champion.

Pascoe might have won the gold, but he simply ran out of time.—**David Coleman**.

I should have won the gold medal at Munich, but I'm glad now I only came third. I'm hard enough to live with as the bronze medallist. With the gold I would have been impossible, and I'd never have realised what a buffoon I was.—**Dwight Stones**.

I was sitting alone in a train when this guy came up and put his hand on my knee. He persisted, so I whapped him one. He did not know what hit him. The police picked him up at the next station.—**Janis Kerr**, English women's shot-putt champion.

1977

Rose's brain will now be telling him exactly what to do.—**Ron Pickering**.

The Irish hammer thrower, Bernie Hartigen, was warming up in the Europa Cup at Copenhagen yesterday. On his first throw his 16 lb hammer smashed a newly installed photo-timing system, hit an official on the head, and missed the judges' table by inches.—*Daily Mail*.

1978

At Crystal Palace the BBC cameras picked up a solemn lady called Paula Fudge as she pounded along a running track with BRITISH MEAT written across her understandably heaving bosom. Sponsorship in sport is one thing but this was altogether a different kettle of offal.—**Dennis Potter**.

When Daley Thompson was winning all those events at Edmonton everyone in our house was cheering like mad at the telly.—**Viv Anderson**.

Those athletes who have been here in Edmonton for five or six days are beginning to open out their legs and show their form. None have shown it better than a Scotsman and an Englishwoman.—**Chris Brasher**, the *Observer*.

1979
There's Harvey Glance, the black American sprinter with the white top and the black bottom.—**Ron Pickering**, BBC.

In my first marathon I got excited, even euphoric. It was a feeling you never got on the track. In a 5,000-metre all they gave you were elbows, on the road competitors hand round sponges.—**Dick Quax**.

Two joggers were stopped by a patrolman in Ohio and charged with using roads 'where paths were available'. They thought the officer was kidding, kept running, and were further charged with resisting arrest. A woman in Colorado was arrested for running through a red traffic light. In Maine another jogger was arrested for littering the highway after throwing an empty can of Energade into a snowbank.—*Sports Illustrated*.

In all my life, in all my meetings with the likes of Nurmi, Owens, Haeg, Zatopek, Kuts, Bannister, Elliott and Snell, I have never met a man like Coe, never been so refreshed by the sanity of a man who can laugh when a radio interviewer tells him he is now an 'all-time great'. I love him for what he has done to destroy the myth and legend of modern sport.—**Chris Brasher**.

My doc recently told me that jogging would add ten years to my life. He was right, I feel ten years older already.—**Milton Berle**.

Finland has produced so many brilliant distance runners because back home it costs $2.50 a gallon for gas.—**Esa Tikkannen**.

1980
I'm on a seafood diet. It means I eat everything I can see.—**Competitor** in New York marathon.

When I lost my world record I took it like a man: I only cried for 10 hours.—**Daley Thompson**.

Oh, do get some gold, it suits you so.—Letter from **Emma Coe** to her brother in Moscow.

The French cannot produce great track and field teams like it can produce great wines for probably that very reason; the winemakers got in first.—**Michel Lourie**, French national coach.

1981
She's dragged the javelin back into the twentieth century.—**Ron Pickering**.

1982
He [Jim Thorpe] was the greatest athlete who ever lived. Lovely fellah. What he had was natural ability. There wasn't anything he couldn't do. All he had to see is someone doin' something and he tried it ... and he'd do it better. He had brute strength ... stamina ... endurance. A lot of times, like in the decathlon, he didn't know what he was doing. He didn't know the right way to throw the javelin or the discus but it didn't matter. He just went there and threw it further than anyone else.—Ninety-year-old **Abel Kiviat**, silver medal winner in the 1912 Olympic Games in Stockholm, recalling the prowess of Jim Thorpe 70 years later.

1983
I didn't run well, but then it was the first day of my period.—**Mary Purcell**, first woman home in the Dublin marathon.

These are two marvellous New Yorkers, but they talk funny.—**Mayor Ed Koch** on NY marathon winners Rod Dixon of New Zealand and Grete Waitz of Norway.

1984

Why runners make lousy communists. In a word, *individuality*. It's the one characteristic all runners, as different as they are, seem to share. . . . Stick with it. Push yourself. Keep running. And you'll never lose that wonderful sense of individuality you now enjoy. Right, comrade?—**Advert** for running shoes in the US, during the Games.

If Carl (Lewis) were to play pro football, he'd have to take a pay cut.—**Joe Douglas** on an unsuccessful approach to Lewis by Dallas Cowboys.

I'll be glad when they eliminate the word amateur from this sport.—**Joe Douglas**, Carl Lewis's business manager.

You can't train the way I do and go out with girls.—**Joaquin Cruz**, churchgoing Baptist, teetotaller and Brazil's Olympic gold medallist in the 800 metres.

In 1980 I was frightened to death of the competition. But I took it like a man, and came back.—**Tessa Sanderson**, Britain's javelin gold medallist.

My god, gas costs so much.—**Orlando Pizzolato**, New York Marathon winner, on hearing prizes included a Mercedes.

1985

The *Daily Mail* keeping her away from any other press was a mistake.—**Peter Labuschagne**, Zola Budd's coach.

Much of the drugtaking in athletics would stop if other athletes were not having to keep up with the American Joneses.—**Sir Arthur Gold**, president of the European Athletics Association.

If I'd been Mary Decker I would have tried to get up and fight back. She owed it to her home crowd.—**Maricica Puica**, Romanian 3,000 metre victor.

1974

Being a manager is simple. All you have to do is keep the five players who hate your guts away from the five who are undecided.—**Casey Sengel**, US baseball manager.

Philadelphia fans would boo a funeral.—Pitcher **Bo Belinsky** on the City of Brotherly Love.

1976

I'm going to write a book, 'How to Make a Small Fortune in Sport'. You start with a large fortune.—**Ruly Carpenter**, president of Philadelphia Phillies.

Baseball has prostituted itself. Pretty soon we'll be starting games at midnight so the people in outer space can watch on prime-time television. We're making a mistake by always going for more money.—San Diego Padres owner and MacDonald hamburger king **Ray Kroc**, reflecting on the October viewing figures for the World Series.

1977

Ninety per cent of baseball is half mental.—**Jim Wohlford**, Milwaukee Brewers outfielder.

We'll win if the Big Dodger in the sky wills it.—Los Angeles manager **Tommy Lasorda** at the outset of the 1977 season.

1984

I've got a face made for radio.—**Ron Luciano**, US baseball umpire, on his failure as NBC-TV summariser.

I don't think I can be expected to take seriously any game which takes less than three days to reach its conclusion.—**Tom Stoppard**, playwright and cricket buff, on baseball in New York.

1985

They belong to baseball.—Commissioner **Peter Ueberooth**, restoring Hall of Fame veterans Mickey Mantle and Willie Mays after banning because of gambling connections.

1971

If I fight a grizzly bear in Red China I'd still draw a full house.—**Muhammad Ali**.

Clay is tender with his punches, lays them on as delicately as you put a postage stamp on an envelope, then cracks them in like a riding crop across your face, strikes a cruel jab like a baseball bat held head-on into your mouth, next waltzes you into a clinch with a tender arm around your neck, wings away out of reach on flying legs, digs a hook with the full swing of a baseball bat hard into your ribs, hard pokes of a jab into your face, a mocking soft flurry of pillows and gloves, a mean forearm cuts you off from coming on him, a cool wrestle of your neck in a clinch, then elusive again, gloves snake lip your face like a whip.—**Norman Mailer**.

Now we're going places.—Manager **Andy Smith**, after Joe Bugner had beaten Henry Cooper.

I resent you calling the matchmaker, Mr Michael Duff, 'my henchman'. He is in fact my 'right-hand man'.—**Mike Barrett**, boxing promoter.

Sure he was awkward, he fell awkwardly.—**Jerry Quarry**, after beating Bodell in 64 seconds.

Get the gun ready, we're going to set traps.—**Muhammad Ali**, immediately after defeat by Frazier.

Frazier is not as ugly as Liston, but there's not much in it.—**Muhammad Ali**.

Well, Jack, at least you won the first round.—**Reporter** to Bodell after Urtain fight.

The referee counted too fast.—**Chuck Olivares** explaining his knock-out by Danny McAlinden.

After sweatin' in fields all day as I did, I'm not goin' to stand for all that Uncle Tom crap.—**Joe Frazier**.

1972

There is blood on my typewriter, blood on my notes, blood on my programme. And however long I live I will never forget the face of Ron Stander standing up to Joe Frazier. The face of courage in tears.—**Peter Wilson**.

A lot of boxing promoters couldn't match the cheeks of their own backside.—**Mickey Duff**, Matchmaker.

Frazier is so ugly that he should donate his face to the US Bureau of Wild Life.—**Muhammad Ali**.

Harry, you're not as dumb as you look.—**Muhammad Ali** to Harry Carpenter.

I know it's said I can't punch but you should see me putting the cat out of a night.—**Chris Finnegan**.

1973

Maybe I am not the greatest British heavyweight champion that ever lived.—**Danny McAlinden**.

When they told me Foreman had beaten Frazier, I thought: My, my. There goes five million dollars.—**Muhammad Ali**.

You can be rich or poor but you don't know nothin' about either until you felt pain.—**Muhammad Ali**.

Jack Solomons was a legend who has now become a myth. He is still a considerable nuisance value, a destructive element, that's all.—**Jarvis Astaire**.

I can't tell you what I really think about Jarvis Astaire because I know the laws of libel too well.—**Jack Solomons**.

I want to rest my bones, rest my body and go lay on some beach and forget this mess. I'll have a £20,000 cheque coming to me every month. Beautiful.—**Muhammad Ali.**

Very modest people often have a great deal to be modest about.—**Jarvis Astaire.**

Any British boxer fighting in Italy has to knock his man out to be even worth a draw.—**Bunny Sterling.**

Should anything go wrong with me now, mentally or physically, I can only blame God. I can only blame something that I can't control.—**Joe Bugner.**

I don't stand there and look at the ball and wiggle the club like Arnold Palmer and them cats. I walk up and hit it about 350 yards. I figure I could drive longer if I ran up and hit it.—**Muhammad Ali.**

I don't have any money. I'm about broke. I can't get any of the money I've won. I'm supposed to have a lot of contenders knocking at my door, but they aren't there.—**George Foreman.**

I retired because I was sick at the lack of control exercised by the Boxing Board. Years ago I warned the secretary that one day one lot was going to walk into his office and send him out for a pot of tea and he would have to go and get it.—**Jim Wicks.**

Whites seem to enjoy seeing black boxers broke. Rolls-Royce are broke. Nixon's broke. What's their excuse? But they still say 'Ain't it terrible that Joe Louis is broke?'—**Muhammad Ali.**

So over to the ringside—Harry Commentator is your carpenter.—**BBC announcer.**

Some years ago I sparred with Frazier. He whacked me four times in the cobblers and didn't say sorry once; he was champion so I had to grin and bear it.—**Joe Bugner.**

1974
To fight in South Africa would be an affront to my family, my country and my integrity.—**John Conteh.**

For ageing boxers, first your legs go. Then your reflexes go. Third your friends go.—**Willie Pep.**

There seems only one way to beat Foreman: shell him for three days and then send the infantry in.—**Hugh McIlvanney**.

Ali fell over the ropes as if he was leaning backwards out of the bathroom window to see if the cat was on the roof.—**George Plimpton**.

1975

If a fighter don't have no defence, he might as well be in a poker game with Doc Kearns without no cards. And he's gotta be mean too, mean like Victor McLaglen cleaning out a saloon in an old John Ford movie.—**Al Braverman**, Chuck Wepner's manager.

Man, I hit him with punches that'd bring down the walls of a city. Lawdy, Lawdy, he's a great champion.—**Joe Frazier**, fighting Muhammad Ali.

It was like death. Closest thing to dyin' that I know of. I was thinking at the end, 'What am I doin' here against this beast of a man'. But after it's all over, now I want to tell the world that he's one helluva man actually, and God bless him.—**Muhammad Ali**, fighting Joe Frazier.

Boxing is probably the best and most individual lifestyle you can have in society without being a criminal.—**Randy Neumann**, US heavyweight.

Just call me a promoter. Not the first black one. Not the first green one. But *the* promoter. There ain't no others.—**Don King**.

Because I would have to raise false hopes back home I have to ... completely dismiss John Stracey's impractical dream of glory.—**Frank McGhee**, *Daily Mirror*.

1976
Boxing is sort of like jazz. The better it is the fewer people can understand it.—**George Foreman**.

One of the many things I like about Stracey as a world champion fighter is that he recognises and realises how ruthless his job must be. He wasn't above hitting Lewis low, or after the bell.—**Frank McGhee**.

One thing I do suffer from is overconfidence. It's something I'm working on.—**George Foreman**.

I dedicate my gold medal to my mother, wherever she may be.—**John-John Davies**, US boxer.

Richard's not overawed by this Ali. Why, we've got far too many of these black chat merchants back 'ome in Bradford. He's right used to seeing them dance up and down Westgate with their tambourines every Saturday.—**Jimmy Devanney**, trainer of Richard Dunn.

C'mon, you guys, let's try and take this thing seriously.
—**Muhammad Ali**, minutes before going out to fight
Richard Dunn.

1977

I knew he was hurt, and that if he did get up he'd be hurt
some more. When you land a good punch you can feel it in
your arm, your shoulder, your hip, your toes, your
toenails.—Heavyweight **Ken Norton**, after knocking out
Duane Bobick 58 seconds into the first round.

I began the poetry and predicting rounds. And it worked.
They started coming with their ten- and twenty-dollar bills
to see the bragging nigger ... How do *I* know who the
greatest fighter was?—**Muhammad Ali**, to a *Los Angeles
Times* reporter.

If you hadn't been there it wouldn't have been much of a
fight.—**Harry Carpenter** to Ken Norton.

1978

They're selling video cassettes of the Ali–Spinks fight for
$89.95. Hell, for that money Spinks will come to your
house.—**Ferdie Pacheco**.

'I had never seen such a display of dancing in the ring,' said Mr Big-Toe Dankovitch, trainer to Harvey Gartley. 'I told Harvey to dance in the first round, sure enough Oulette never landed a punch. But Harvey overdid it. He danced himself into exhaustion and collapsed unconscious after 47 seconds.' Oulette won on a technical knockout.—**Christopher Logue**, *South China Post*.

I felt more then [after defeating Ken Norton] than when I got the decision in Las Vegas. I was so happy I thought I was gonna cry. But I kept things in, and I just waved. It wouldn't be right for a world heavyweight champion to be crying.—**Larry Holmes**, after beating Ken Norton in their world heavyweight championship fight.

1979

Hey, in that film Rocky, the black bum says 'I'll kill him, I'm the Master of Disaster!' Master of Disaster! Greece, I wish I'd thought of that!—**Muhammad Ali**.

My wife keeps saying 'I'm in my study'. The only thing I study in there is the Beano.—**John Conteh**.

Did it hurt? Of course it did. You'd hurt too, mate, if you'd just been belted one by a flamin' world champion.
—**John Conteh**.

The first BBC Grandstands I used to watch at home with my father. He was particularly keen on boxing. It was a joke in the family that he always had to have sausage and mash for Saturday lunch so he didn't have to look down watching 'Fight of the Week'. While sitting there he used to say to me 'You could do that job'.—**Frank Bough**.

If going through your life you meet more than one Jim Watt then you're a lucky man. He's such a stand up-fella. He's been around a long time and you've never heard one bad thing said about him.—**Terry Lawless.**

I'm still the best heavyweight fighter in Canada and I'll still be the best when I'm dead seven years.—**George Chuvalo.**

1980
My mind wasn't on the fight in the first round and I didn't realise I had been knocked down.—**Charlie Magri.**

Whenever I'm away from Derry for more than two or three days I am desperate to get back. And I've never got home and it hasn't been raining.—**Charlie Nash.**

No, I don't mind the fight being at three in the morning. Everyone in Glasgow fights at three in the morning.—**Jim Watt.**

His best weapon is his chin.—**Richie Giachetti,** Marvin Hagler's manager, speaking about former middleweight champ Vito Antuofermo.

It's bad enough losing, but to get up in the morning, hurt, and read that you're just a club fighter or a journeyman, that hurts.—**Sandy LeDoux**, heavyweight Scott LeDoux's wife. LeDoux fought Holmes, Foreman, Ken Norton, Mike Weaver, and Duane Bobick.

When I go along for a quiet evening's entertainment throwing beer cans I do not expect my enjoyment to be ruined by the sight of two grown men beating the living daylights out of each other.—Letter to the *Guardian* from **Paul Skirrow**.

Throughout the fight I was trying to pump him up. But you can't pump up a torn tyre, just like you can't get water out of a dry well.—**Angelo Dundee**, Muhammad Ali's trainer.

I know I should not do it, many people say I should not do it, but it's a risk and what I would gain is immortality, four times world heavyweight champion. Two times world champion is great, three times is great, but a four-time heavyweight champion of the world, I'll be the greatest athlete of all times, not just a boxer.—**Muhammad Ali**, coming out of retirement at 38. Larry Holmes beat him easily.

No mas, no mas, no more box.—**Roberto Duran**, abruptly ending his second fight with Sugar Ray Leonard in the 8th round, due to stomach cramps. He had eaten two 16-ounce steaks for dinner, and a further steak for dessert.

What helped me develop my quickness was fear. I think the rougher the opponent, the quicker I am.—**Sugar Ray**

Leonard, just before his second fight with Roberto Duran.

1981
Born in Italy, most of his fights have been in his native New York.—**Des Lynam**.

1982
Magri has to really do well against this unknown Mexican who comes from that famous family of five brothers.—**Harry Carpenter**.

Gerry Cooney is understated, gentle, sensitive, understanding and real without momentarily compromising his macho.—His manager, **Dennis Rappaport**.

The Mexicans, these tiny little men from South America.—**Harry Carpenter**.

1983
Hagler uses his bald head as a third hand. I'm a far cleaner fighter. He should be grateful I'm making him so much money. He wouldn't get $10 million for fighting anybody else.—**Roberto Duran**.

Everyone knows Duran has been the dirtiest fighter around for years. That's what he does best, and that's what makes him so dangerous.—**Marvin Hagler**.

There's no way an amateur with 10 fights can beat me. This kid should be sucking a bottle.—**Larry Holmes** before beating Marvis Frazier in Round One.

1984

I'm going to Russia to fight Gerrie Coetzee for $20 million.—**Muhammad Ali**, still kidding.

I'm behind Terry Lawless 210 per cent.—**Frank Bruno** after boxing cartel allegations.

I wish they'd feed me some of the bums they hand out to those boys. Every time I step into the ring I face a war.—**Pat Cowdell**, super-featherweight, on Frank Bruno and Erroll Christie.

I'm grateful for what I've got, but I'm a clumsy git really.—**Tony Sibson**, before a fight with Mark Kaylor.

I never cease to amaze myself. I say this humbly.—**Don King**, US boxing promoter.

All fighters are prostitutes and all promoters are pimps.—**Larry Holmes**.

1985

I would not put my life on the line for a measly million dollars.—Heavyweight champion **Larry Holmes** before his 47th victory against David Bey.

I don't know why he was so upset with himself. I landed some good punches.—**Barry McGuigan**, after defending his European featherweight title against Farid Gallouze of France.

1971

Shall we put our heads down and make runs or get out quickly and make history.—**Peter Walker** greeting Don Shepherd at the wicket with Glamorgan 11 for 8 against Leicestershire.

Chandrasekhar bowled well, but he wasn't exactly turning the ball square, was he? In fact he was hardly turning the ball at all.—**Farokh Engineer**, India's wicketkeeper.

Knott and Engineer are probably the happiest Test cricketers in the business.—**Brian Scovell**.

Try explaining cricket to an intelligent foreigner; it is far harder than explaining Chomsky's generational grammar.—**C. P. Snow**.

Sir Learie Constantine belongs to that rare and tiny group of athletes whose deeds are not printed in record books but burned on the mind. We shall miss him, except when we remember him, when he was in his prime and beautiful.—**Michael Parkinson**.

If I can see 'em I can hit 'em.—Lancashire's **David Hughes** at 9 p.m. before scoring 24 in an over to win a Gillette Cup semifinal.

I am still badly feeling the effect of my injury and will not be returning to the Yorkshire side for some time.—**Geoff Boycott**, after scoring 138 not out in a club match for Leeds.

I find I am playing every ball, bowling every ball and fielding every ball. The captaincy has cost me over 600 runs a season. I am snapping at my wife and children and sleeping no more than four hours a night.—**Mickey Stewart**, captain of Surrey, the county champions.

Come on. No, wait! Get back. . . . Sorry!—**Geoff Boycott**.

1972
Marsh might hit sixes, but he is not a slogger. I would call him a Very Scientific Hard Hitter.—**Jack Fingleton**.

Dark clouds are coming up from the south-west—and I'm sorry to tell you that the wind is blowing in the same direction.—**Brian Johnston**.

I've never been a good professional cricketer ... I'm bloody marvellous for three days on the trot, very good for another day, but, in terms of concentration, not so hot for the next two or three.—**Tony Lewis**.

If my mother hadn't thrown my football boots on the fire I might have become as famous as Denis Compton.—**Len Hutton**.

When cricketers scowl and chew gum the result is highly unattractive. But Barry Richards completes a perfect technical picture of bland assurance unmarred by a rotating jaw.—**E. W. Swanton**.

My dad's greatest claim to fame is that he went to school with John Arlott.—**Graham Roope**.

1973

Football has become a vast bore. Sports editors and producers, who have so often allowed key space to be occupied by football trivia, because of cricket's weakness back in the sixties, may soon have to think again. Cricket has for the moment the priceless gift of variety.—**Robin Marlar**.

I am not unhappy to be hit for six sixes. I want batsmen to play shots. Only then I can get them out!—**Bishen Bedi.**

I'll never be accepted by some of the snob press.—**Ray Illingworth.**

E. W. Swanton—Sort of a Cricket Peron.—**Headline in Jamaica.**

The severest criticism of Ray Illingworth is that he did not sufficiently discourage the element of selfishness which is part of most successful cricketers.—**Mike Brearley.**

1974

It's a privilege to be hit by Sobers for six, better even than to bowl 20 dreary maidens on the trot to Geoff Boycott.—**Bishen Bedi.**

BRING BACK WARD!—*Sun*, northern edition, Aug. 16.
BRING BACK SNOW!—*Sun*, southern edition, Aug. 16.

To dismiss this lad Denness you don't have to bowl fast, you just have to run up fast.—**Brian Close.**

I enjoy hitting a batsman more than getting him out. I like to see blood on the pitch. And I've been training on whisky.—**Jeff Thomson**.

The Australian Government should deport the English geriatrics now posing as cricketers. And the MCC should be charged with fraud under the Trade Practices Act.—**Barry Cohen**, Labour MP.

How can sports page cricket be so good and literary cricket so bad? And cricket is made for a musical. I can see the Cecil Beaton costumes now.—**Stanley Reynolds.**

There's no style left in cricket, no individuality. Players should wear numbers on their backs now so you can tell them apart.—**Trevor Howard.**

Most cricket critics, who have more power than any other writers in sport, would see Chairman Mao as British Prime Minister before they would give Boycott the vote as England's captain.—**Ian Wooldridge.**

If I'd gone to Cambridge or Oxford there'd have been no limits to what I could've achieved.—**Geoffrey Boycott.**

During the first Test, when Colin had no idea he'd been called for, I was waking up every few minutes to try to find out the score. And I found this station that gave the total every hour, and Colin insisted that I woke him up every time to tell him the score.—**Mrs Penny Cowdrey**.

You would think that this English Test team was in a holiday camp. Their dining room has high chairs for the players' children and on mornings of tough Tests are England's heroes popping cornflakes into their youngsters' mouths. In Brisbane and Sydney it was absurd to call these men with bats batsmen; they were weak-kneed imposters.—**Keith Miller**.

1975

This miners' strike is ridiculous. There's tea ladies at the top of the mine who are earning more than county cricketers. Arthur Scargill ought to come down here and try bowling 20 overs.—**Ray Illingworth**.

Most county cricketers play the game for the life rather than the living. For them it's the motorways of England rather than the jet lanes of the world. It's sausage, egg, and chips at Watford Gap rather than vol-au-vent and small talk on the Governor-General's lawns in Barbados.—**Michael Carey**.

Keith Fletcher has been on trial longer than the late Caryl Chessman.—**Alan Watkins**.

In the Tests I sometimes break out into a sweat just putting on me boots. You'd be really surprised at how many players are nervous out there.—**Mike Hendrick**.

Was it cosmic tragedy when somebody dug up the Test pitch with a knife and fork? Why couldn't they have moved the thing a yard or two? Elaborate explanations in *The Times* about the arcane conventions of this dotty game in no way persuade me that a just-possibly unjust prison sentence of 20 years isn't more important.—**James Cameron**.

G. BOYCOTT IS INNOCENT OK.—Jon's Headingley daub.

Lord Hawke probably took the same view as I do about families on tour with the MCC players. It is no more a place for them than a trench on the Somme.—**John Woodcock**.

My son bought a new cricket ball. On it in gold lettering it said 'Gunn and Moore, Ltd., Nottingham' with 'England' added for good measure. Underneath in tiny letters, not in gold, indeed hardly visible at all, the words 'Made in India' are stamped.—**Alan Watkins**.

The MCC's new tactical plan is for them to take a single in the middle of each over, so that each batsman can have a respite from the bumper barrage.—*London Evening News*.

There's only one head bigger than Tony Greig—and that's Birkenhead.—**Fred Trueman**.

He looked good, was good, and by golly he did us good.—**Mrs Mary Chapman**, farmer's wife, winning a David Steele competition.

I have one special memory of this year's Gillette. In the semifinal at Old Trafford between Lancashire and Gloucestershire . . . Foat's magnificent boundary catch to dismiss Clive Lloyd was the signal for the whole Gloucester side to descend on Foat at long leg. For David Shepherd, fielding at deep mid-on, this meant a long journey, but he set off, like a great steam engine, whistle going, flywheel spinning, rods flashing, earth shaking. Decorated, it seemed, with brass and copper, he thundered past the Railway Stand, arriving long after everyone else to shake Foat by the hand.—**John Woodcock**.

Football managers don't look on county cricketers as professionals, but just because they enjoy themselves they are no less professional. There is more comradeship in cricket and nowhere near so much back-stabbing as in football. Cricketers always accept defeat, footballers cannot.—**Jim Cumbes**, Aston Villa and Worcestershire.

When television voices at the Tests do surface, it is their timbre rather than idiom which grips—a speech therapist's dream: Ray Illingworth (it's not a pulling wicket, this isn't), the twanging 'eows' and 'ois' that punctuate Denis Compton's carefully reclaimed accent, and Jim Laker's pronunciation is as canny as his old tweakers—if he can say swingin', why does he say innins, and why doesn't he say swinnin'?—**Martin Amis**, *New Statesman*.

The England team to meet Australia in the first Test is: Denness, Knott, Cowdrey, Underwood, Luckhurst, Woolmer, Nicholls, Ealham, Johnson, Graham, and Asif Iqbal (Hyderabad, near Beckenham, Kent); 12th Man: Fuller Pilch.—**Michael Parkinson**.

1976

Brian Toss won the close.—**Henry Blofeld** on Radio 2.

While English cricketers have laboured and lumbered and been seen to commit the elemental sin of fretting in public, the West Indies have displayed all the qualities once seen essential to the ambitious young District Commissioner.—**Ian Wooldridge**.

Sir.—So the Home Secretary has no power to ban this foreign director coming here to make a film showing Jesus in the nude, drinking and love-making. Yet no such problem arose when the Government wanted to ban a Rhodesian cricket team.—Letter in *Daily Telegraph*.

Johnson, at 29 a fine batsman and offspinner, seems eminently suitable to be Kent's captain. He is a thoughtful and intelligent cricketer who must have made many followers of cricket less suspicious of the products of the London School of Economics.—*Daily Telegraph* leader.

The last batsman, Albeit Carefully, survived till lunch.—*Hawkes Bay Gazette*.

Truly, I think I could get more runs if England had some faster bowlers.—**Vivian Richards**.

As cricket surges down the years, the mathematical cherish its statistics. But the literary relish its sharp Saxon vocab.: drive, block, cut, glance, pull, spin, toss, lob, swing, not to mention its silly mid-offs and deep square-legs.—**John F. X. Harriott**.

If Greig fell off the Empire State Building, he'd land in a passing furniture van filled with mattresses.—**England cricketer**.

1977

It says here, Mr Pele, that you have shaken hands with the Pope. I take it you are referring to Mr George Pope, the balding former Derbyshire right hand bowler.—**Bill Grundy**.

I like the Stylistics and the Carpenters. I also like going to the ballet, and sometimes take my mum.—**Geoffrey Boycott**.

In his century at Headingley, Boycott touched the ankle of his right foot 40 times each hour. He took off his cap and wiped his brow 364 times. He played 466 balls. He marks his guard twice every time he gets down to the business end, one at the usual mark, the other inside his crease.—**Jack Fingleton**.

Of the three Yorkshiremen who have scored 100 hundreds, the most beautiful player, by far, was Hutton. The man to play an innings for your life was Sutcliffe. The man to play an innings for his own life is Boycott.—**Alan Gibson**.

Come on, we are all harlots—it is all a matter of price.
How much do you fellows want?—**Kerry Packer**.

I was so impressed with Mr Boycott's conduct on your
show on Saturday that I intend writing to the
Director-General asking if we can see more of Geoffrey
Boycott on our screens in future. And less of you.—**Letter**
to Michael Parkinson.

There have been various occasions since he became an
England cricketer when Greig has overplayed his hand. ...
What has to be remembered of course is that he is not an
Englishman by birth or upbringing, but only by adoption.
It is not the same thing as being English through and
through.—**John Woodcock**, *The Times*.

Cricket is a situation game. When the situation is dead, the
game is dead.—**Trevor Bailey**.

I have nightmares about having to become an
umpire.—**John Snow**.

1978

Gower is a different class. His bat is such an extension of his arms and wrists that the blade often appears to be flexible.—**H. F. Ellis.**

When we were living in Sydney a friend told me that one night, while she and her husband were making love, she suddenly noticed something sticking in his ear. When she asked him what it was he replied 'Be quiet! I'm listening to the cricket'.—**Vicky Rantzen**, the *Observer*.

Boycott might be the harder man to get out, but I have never known it suggested that anyone in his own side has deliberately run Brearley out.—**Alan Gibson.**

And umpire Dickie Bird is gestating wildly as usual.—**Tony Lewis**, BBC.

C'mon the Whites!—**bored cricket watcher.**

When Randall was run out backing-up in New Zealand I thought that if that had been at my school the bowler would have been beaten for it by a housemaster—and quite right too.—**Phil Edmonds.**

When I left Yorkshire I received a letter from the secretary saying they were not going to offer me a contract which began: 'Dear Ray Illingworth...' But they had crossed the 'Ray' out. They couldn't even bring themselves to call me by my first name or use a fresh piece of paper.—**Ray Illingworth.**

For the capacity to enliven a dull game, to bring a sleepy public to life; for bouts of furious, violent athleticism channelled through control, and interspersed with spells of amusingly haughty impassivity; for taking the whole thing as seriously as his watchers want him to, but not a touch of anguish more—I think it would be hard to beat the cricketer, Viv Richards.—**Russell Davies**.

Thursday: Mudassar, given out lbw, was furious when he returned to the changing-room. He said: 'That's the end of cricket for me. I think I'll start running a discotheque.'—**Wasim Bari's diary**, quoted by Dudley Doust, *Sunday Times*.

It was Ludwig Wittgenstein who first made me interested in cricket when he said in the Logico-Absurdicus that 'everything of which we cannot speak is a lot of balls', said Mike Borely, England's captain. 'When I am waiting for Lillee to bowl I find myself humming the second subject from the adagio furioso third movement of Haydn's op. 74 string quartet, better known to music lovers as "the Duck", which is what I usually score.'—**Lord Gnome**.

In Mike Brearley's unarrogant flat, where he lives alone—rumpled bedclothes in mid-afternoon and unwashed plates on the kitchen table—I made a beeline for the bookshelves. I spotted *Games People Play, The Divided Self, Human Aggression, The Art of Loving, Perspectives in Group Therapy, The Miracle Worker, The Poems of Auden*. I wonder what books Greig and Boycott have on their shelves?—**David Benedictus**.

Graves is likely to be out for a month with a broken index finger on his bottom hand.—**Robin Marlar**, *Sunday Times*.

Ted Heath is the Geoff Boycott of politics—he doesn't like to play unless he can be captain. But the comparison is unfair to Boycott. In the first place Boycott in many ways is a modest and unassuming man. In the second, he has a great loyalty to his county. And in the third, he makes a hell of a lot of runs. Heath rarely makes any runs, and always ends knocking down all his stumps.—**Paul Johnson.**

Why are the umpires the only two people on a cricket field who aren't going to get grass stains on their knees, the only ones allowed to wear dark trousers?—**Katharine Whitehorn.**

1979

Some time ago I asked Ian Botham whether he had always been an aggressive sportsman. He shamelessly revealed that he often used to get sent off when he was playing Under-11s football at school.—**Mike Brearley.**

The amazing thing about Procter is that he goes out with any bat he picks up; he never worries about the weight, balance or pick-up of a bat; he just goes out there and hammers it.—**Brian Brain.**

If you hired Mr Arlott to stand (preferably sit) in a ploughed field, it would eventually come to be seen as a cricket pitch. Sooner or later, men would turn up with planks and start building a pavilion.—**Russell Davies**.

Sir—The scoreline 'Lillee c Willey b Dilley' brings to mind similar combinations. In 1972 we had Colley bowling to Dolly, Lillee to Illy, and Greg (Chappell) to Greig. (These personal duels can be quoted in reverse order.) In the 1960s we may have had Kettle (Northants) bowling to Kitchen (Somerset). Between the wars two of Notts' wicketkeepers were Oates and Wheat. In Nottingham there is a firm of estate agents called Turner, Fletcher & Essex.—Letter in *Wisden Monthly*.

As I stood at the non-strikers end, I felt a wave of admiration for my partner; wiry, slight, dedicated, a lonely man doing a lonely job all these years. What is it that compels Geoffrey Boycott to prove himself again and again among his peers?—**Mike Brearley**.

When I bowled at Graveney, Dexter or Cowdrey, I'd expect the ball to be clattered back at my shins faster than I bowled it. That never happens today against English batsmen.—**David Brown**, Warwickshire.

'Twas evenin' time in t'Vatican, and t'Pope 'ad gone t'bed.
'E wor laid there reading Penthouse wi' 'is skullcap on
  'is 'ead.
Then rhand about ten-thirty a knock came at front door
An' there stood a tiny errand boy all breathless an' footsore.
'E stood there, eyes all wet wi' tears, 'is voice abaht t'crack:
'Tha'd best raise t' gaffer right away, Geoff Boycott's got
  the sack!'
—Poem in *Guardian* by **D. Cleaver**, Oldham.

The obvious successor to Brearley at the moment isn't
obvious.—**Trevor Bailey**, BBC.

What Connors and Nastase do are calculated stratagems to
help them win a tennis match. What Randall does on a
cricket field is no more than an urchin's wish to delight
and cast gloom away.—**Geoffrey Moorhouse**.

The umpire is one of cricket's richest inventions. He is in
fact a figure of such metaphysical and religious profundity
that he not only takes on but embodies the mystery of
things. If it is said that cricket is the key to life (as I often
do), equally it can be said that the umpire is the key to
cricket.—**John F. X. Harriott**.

Collis King has been banned from the North Wales
League because he is 'too good'. He played for Pontblyddn
(pop. 200), near Mold. In 12 innings his average was 139
(74 sixes, 92 fours). The result of one match was
Pontblyddn 391 for 7 (King 283 not out); St Asaph 11 and
30 (King 6 for 2).—**Paul Foot**, *New Statesman.*

Looking back on all my years as an umpire I'd say my ideal
and happiest games were those involving Essex and
Lancashire, and my least ideal those in which Somerset or
Leicestershire were playing.—**Jack Crapp**.

I drove 14,500 miles this summer and that's a lot of service
stations, map checks and listening to my Gloucestershire
companion, David Partridge, snoring his permed head off.
When we play at Bristol I drive 136 miles a day from my
home in Worcester. I hope Partridge stays awake a little
longer next season: I get bored picking my World XI by
myself.—**Brian Brain**.

1980

In affectionate remembrance of English Cricket which
died at Lord's on September 2, 1980, aged one hundred.
The body will be re-cremated and sent to the home of
bureaucracy, officialdom, and the tactics of defensive,
unadventurous cricket.—Letter in *Wisden Cricket
Monthly*.

On Saturday May 27 at Headingley, Yorkshire dismissed
Lancashire at 12.47 p.m. for 123, the innings having lasted
for 27.1 overs. Is this the highest score any side has been
dismissed for before lunch on the first day of a county
match?—Letter in *Wisden Cricket Monthly*.

Clive Lloyd's West Indians would have given Bradman's 1948 'unbeatables' a real run for their money. We'd have won, but only just.—**Neil Harvey**.

Sir,—An electrician recently came into my office to mend the fire alarm. Finding a broken wire he said, 'Look at this, it's kerried.' I asked what he meant, and he replied, 'It's Kerry Packered—knackered!'—Letter in *Wisden Cricket Monthly*.

Deryk Murray has batted well: he is the nigger in the woodpile as far as the English are concerned.—**Brian Johnston**.

And we welcome listeners back to Lord's with the news that steady fighting is continuing in the Long Room and that there will be a further inspection of the pitch at 2.45 when umpire Constant returns from his psychiatrist.—**Lord Gnome**.

1981
The BBC did not apologise to viewers who were deprived of seeing half of Botham's century on Saturday at Old Trafford because somebody in his wisdom decided precedence should be taken by a horserace from Newbury and the Midland Bank Horse Trials.—**Richard Ingrams**.

Now Botham's coming on, with a chance to put everything that's gone before behind him.—**Tony Cozier**.

It is all just physically and mentally soul destroying.—**Geoffrey Boycott**.

It was Jung, I think, who said we learned from our failures, success merely confirming us in our mistakes. What can I learn from my batting failures at Test level?—**Mike Brearley**.

Judgments by commentators should be made on probability, not outcome. So when Jim Laker writes in the *Express* on Friday that it was a mistake to put Australia in to bat at The Oval, one should know that his opinion (given to Paul Parker's father) an hour before the start on Thursday was that we should field. And it is facile to refer to playing only four specialist bowlers as 'folly' only after three of them have broken down.—**Mike Brearley**.

Well, there's only one thing I can say after that over, and that's to clap my hands.—**Trevor Bailey**.

1982
I was cheered, of course, by Mr May's phone call, but at once I felt a deep sadness for Keith Fletcher. Then immediately there was another call: it was from the Gnome, deep in the Essex countryside: 'Good luck, Goose, don't worry about me, I'll be all right.'—**Bob Willis** (after his appointment as England captain).

We are very happy to be in Sri-Lon.—**Keith Fletcher**.

In attaining his world record Mr Boycott has occupied the creases of the world for 75 full days.—**Bill Frindall**.

Then there was that dark horse with the golden arm, Mudassar Nazar.—**Trevor Bailey**.

When I toured South Africa with Oxbridge Jazzhats, I became physically ill after a week. We were being used for propaganda. I will never return there.—**Derek Pringle**.

When you dream, as I did last night, that you've been picked to open the batting for MCC in Australia and come the great day you can't find your bat, you don't really need Freud or the Maudsley Hospital to give you clues as to the balance in your mental account.—**Jeffrey Bernard**.

1983

The greatest tragedy of his troubled life is that, above all else, in the desire to be admired and loved by everyone, he has this enormous capacity for upsetting people.—**Tony Greig** on Boycott.

I'll send the Scunthorpe lads a telegram, urging them to stay in the Cup until I get back from Pakistan. I've checked it out ... on April 14 they should be in the semi-finals which will allow me a couple of weeks to get back into shape after the tour.—**Ian Botham**.

They've always had a lot of talent. But they're like 11 women. You know, scratching each other's eyes out and wanting to do this and that. That's always been their downfall as a team.—**Botham** on Pakistan.

Obviously there were some disagreements between the two (Boycott and Illingworth). But they have now got to the stage where they are prepared to play cricket with each other. As long as there's in-fighting within the club, we are not going to get anywhere.—**Michael Crawford**, Yorkshire chairman, before the season.

Wouldn't it make more sense if I just got in the fridge?—**Qasim Omar**, Pakistan batsman, who needed six ice-packs on wounds inflicted by Australia's bowlers.

I think we can beat these blokes more often than not. They are a bit past it. I mean, poor old Lillee trudging around out there. He should be out to grass long since.—**Prime Minister Robert Muldoon** on New Zealand's trip to Australia.

There are some things about Ian Chappell I shouldn't have copied, like the way he always used to refuse to sign autographs in a bar. Here was me, 18, telling 50-year-olds to stuff off.—**David Hookes**.

I reckon I sent two fans to hospital at the end of the England–New Zealand game at The Oval. I worked on a dockside for 30 years and I know how to dish it out if I need to.—**Don Oslear**, Test umpire, after brandishing a stump at pitch-invaders at Old Trafford.

Roger Knight is a smashing bloke, but he's no captain. I asked him if I could do some bowling again and all I got was two balls when the other team needed two to win.—**David Smith**, after resigning from Surrey.

The decision (to sack Boycott) had to be made—and it should've been made 10 years ago.—**Fred Trueman**.

I don't know of another club in history which finished bottom of the league, sacked its star player and left the manager in the job. The Yorkshire committee are guilty of the biggest whitewash I can ever recall.—**Brian Clough** on the sacking of Boycott.

We must be the only working-class family in Western Australia who have gone ex-directory.—**Bill Donnison**, whose son, Gary, was the victim of the citizen's arrest that cost Australia the services of Terry Alderman.

I've been swamped by letters from ordinary Yorkshire members who can't contain their outrage. I've heard from others whose children won't stop crying because they'll never see Geoff bat again at Headingley or Scarborough.—**Sid Fielden**, Barnsley policeman and pro-Boycott organiser.

1984
When there's a hosepipe ban covering three-quarters of the country, you don't expect a damp wicket at Lord's.—**Bob Willis**, Warwickshire captain, on his side's Benson & Hedges final defeat.

This is a Test match. It's not Old Reptonians versus Lymeswold, one off the mark and jolly good show.—**David Gower**, England captain, declining to criticise Malcolm Marshall for bowling bouncers in fifth Test.

To offer Geoff Boycott a new contract is akin to awarding Arthur Scargill the Queen's Award for Industry.—Letter in the *Yorkshire Post*.

I would like him to resign but I don't think there's an earthly chance of his doing so.—**Sid Fielden**, pro-Boycott leader last winter, in November, on Boycott's dual role as player and committee man.

Team morale is sky high.—**Bob Merriman**, Australian cricket manager, before second Test defeat which forced resignation—and tears—from Kim Hughes.

Without being unkind, a donkey could lead West Indies at the moment. But put Clive Lloyd in charge of Australia and even he'd struggle.—**Keith Fletcher**, ex-England skipper, after Hughes's resignation from captaincy.

1985

Sport is a means of providing pleasure to people—it is like offering clothes to those who need them.—**Abdul Rahman Bukhatir**, Arabian promoter of the Asia Cup.

It is a sign of the times perhaps that high on the agenda of the Test and County Cricket Board's Spring meeting are drugs, drink, hooliganism and bad language.—**Paul Fitzpatrick**.

Since the England players arrived on 31 October India had the assassination of its Prime Minister and a British diplomat 24 hours after he entertained us, thousands of deaths in communal slaughter, the Bhopal disaster, the world's most elaborate democratic exercise and a spy scandal. One morning in New Zealand the main item on the morning news concerned a fisherman trying to land a large marlin.—**Matthew Engel**.

1971

It would be wrong for me to disclose how much
showjumpers earn since it could bring about Inland
Revenue problems.—**Jack Webber**, British Show Jumping
secretary.

Ken Buchanan has been voted sportsman of the year by the
Sports Writers' Association. The women's award went to
horsewoman Anne Elizabeth Alice Louise Windsor.
—News item, *Morning Star*.

1973

You cameramen are getting my goat. Horses are very
sensitive. They are not like humans. They don't
understand what all the fuss is about.—**Princess Anne**.

Hello and welcome to this great week of show-jumping, and as I say in this week of show-jumping we won't be seeing show-jumping, we'll be seeing all the people who make show-jumping such a spectacle this week, this week of show-jumping in which, as I say, the 49 qualifiers for tonight's event have been simmered down to those 21 people who'll make this night of show-jumping not just part of this great week of show-jumping we've been looking forward to as I say, but the people who, the people who...—**David Vine**, BBC commentator.

1974
If I get a £5 speeding fine it's all over the front pages. If I win the Grand Prix of Rotterdam, one of the greatest of all titles, the back pages don't even mention it.—**Harvey Smith**.

Girls who ride horses don't necessarily have big behinds.—**Ann Moore**.

1975
The Ann Moore engagement was the sort of sick period for me, and the court case was just awful. When you have real problems, you can go and bury yourself with your horses. They are very forgiving and comforting at times like that.—**David Broome**.

1976
I mean, fame's quite fun and all that, but as soon as anything goes wrong or you make a big bog of something, everyone knows about it, and that does *taint* it a bit.—**Lucinda Prior-Palmer**.

One does tend to go on a bit about horses, doesn't one?—**Princess Anne**.

1979

The transition from riding a pony to riding a horse is difficult, because they're, of course, totally different animals.—**Lucinda Prior-Palmer**.

1982

Sandra Denault, 17, broke her ankle in two places when she landed after jumping for the Royal Association for Disability and Rehabilitation on Saturday.—*Salisbury Journal*.

Even among the horsey fraternity, I imagine viewers are fairly cheesed off watching those same old riders, Harvey Smith, Schockemole *et al*, going over the same old fences on the same old horses night after night. And not just this week, but all through the year. It has become an advertising racket with a lot of people doing very well out of it.—**Richard Ingrams**.

1971

My Grandad said the only way to forget about a woman is find another one.—**Lee Trevino**.

Very calm person make very good putt. Me try to be very calm. If I hear bird sing it's no good. Must think only of ball in hole. On the green, not bird and me. Only me. That makes very good putt.—**Lu Liang Huan**.

Trousers are now allowed to be worn by ladies on the course. But they must be removed before entering the clubhouse.—Notice in Irish golf club.

English is difficult. I speak only Hong Kong golf English. When I go to professional I take teacher, say must speak English. Every day it is A-B-C-D, A-B-C-D. But no A-B-C-D in golf, only 1-2-3-4, maybe 5. So I take another teacher.—**Lu Liang Huan**.

1972

A distinguished professor of pathology, who recently holed out in one at the fourth at Walton Heath, thus opening the round with 4371444, asks whether he is the only man in history to have started a round of golf with his own telephone number.—**Henry Longhurst**.

1973

People see my swing and say: 'Oh what a beautiful swing,' and I always want to reply: 'Yeah, but why doesn't it work better?'—**Tommy Aaron**.

On the golf course, unlike films, when you are good and ready, you hit it. And when you have made a mess of it, there is absolutely nobody to blame but yourself, your own greed and your own stupidity. To me it has a pure practical, quasi-religious quality about it. Ultimate total responsibility.—Film director, **Guy Hamilton**.

Someone said that no one 'murders' Troon. The way I played the Open they couldn't even arrest me for second degree manslaughter.—**Lee Trevino**.

I never hit a shot, even in practice, without having a very sharp, in-focus picture of it in my head. It's like a colour movie. First I 'see' the ball where I want it to finish. ... Then the scene quickly changes and I 'see' the ball going there. ... Then there's a sort of fade-out, and the next scene shows me making the kind of swing that will turn the previous images into reality.—**Jack Nicklaus**.

Arnold Palmer used to throw a club now and then. So did I. But now I never blame the course or the caddies or the galleries. When I play rotten golf now I only blame myself. You see I'm a perfectionist.—**Tom Weiskopf.**

We always considered it a feat to sink our six-to-eight-foot putts, but now, if a fellow misses from 40 feet, he grimaces and agonises like a cowboy struck in the heart by an arrow.—**Ben Hogan.**

I have to play bloody well for months in the US to earn $100,000 and then half of that goes to taxes and expenses. I can make more in Europe and go to more exciting places. In the US every tournament seems like the same place.—**Tony Jacklin.**

Winning is a drug. Once you have experienced it, you cannot do without it. You live for it.—**Bernard Hunt.**

1974
Ten times or so in my career I have experienced a state where everything is pure, vividly clear. I'm in a cocoon of concentration, and I'm invincible.—**Tony Jacklin.**

They say some men are good putters or good chippers. Nonsense. The whole secret of golf is to choose the right club for the right shot.—**Gary Player**.

The unfairest thing in golf is the two stroke out-of-bounds penalty: if you shy away and play it safe, you can get by; but if you stand up and play it like a man you can be in real trouble.—**Tony Jacklin**.

1975
I wish I had enough money to do nothing but fly my plane, play a little golf, and go walking in woods.—**Arnold Palmer**.

I tee the ball high because years of experience have shown me that air offers less resistance than dirt.—**Jack Nicklaus**.

Serenity is knowing that your worst shot is still going to be pretty good.—**Johnny Miller**.

Did you ever consider hitting it closer to the hole?—**Ben Hogan**, to a fellow player throwing putting tantrums.

1976
It is still embarrassing for me to play on the US golf circuit. Like the time I asked my caddie for a sand wedge and he comes back ten minutes later with a ham on rye.—**Chi Chi Rodriguez**, Puerto Rican golfer.

I'd give up golf like a shot. It's just that I've got so many sweaters.—**Bob Hope**.

There's a cold war on the women's golf circuit with we straights trying to put down the image of the lesbians. We criticise their dress, mannerisms, and speech. We're losing sponsorship over it. They should go straight for the sake of all of us.—**Carole Mann**.

I'm no good unless I hit over 300 balls a day. You may not see me at the tournament because I practise at a different course. I tell the guys I haven't picked up a stick in weeks, but that's a bunch of bull. I'd go nuts if I didn't hit the balls.—**Lee Trevino**.

The Rules of Golf for Good Players Whose Scores Would Reflect Their True Ability If Only They Got an Even Break Once In a While.—US book title.

I've got a Ford Pantera, a Porsche Carrera, a Mercedes Roadster, a De Tomaso Mangusta, another Porsche, another Mercedes, a station wagon, and a jeep. I guess I'm a nut about cars. I've also got a one-iron. And if I ever broke that little one-iron, that'd be the death in the family.—**Johnny Miller**.

When I play a round with the Mormon Miller, I must always remind myself never to talk about birds or booze.—**Jack Newton**.

1977
I don't like to watch golf on television because I just can't stand people who whisper.—**Dave Brenner**, US comedian.

Golfer Andy North's sister, Pamela, yesterday married Mr Dick South.—UPI report.

I can tell you now that I'll know exactly when I want to retire; but when I reach that time I may not know.—**Jack Nicklaus**.

My golf game's gone off so much that when I went fishing a couple of weeks ago my first cast missed the lake.—**Ben Crenshaw**.

They call women's pro golf the Bitchy Bitch circuit; it's more like the Butchy Butch. They don't seem to have separate dinner dates or anything. They all stick together in their groups and if two of the girls who've paired off have a row, the atmosphere is terrible.—**Julie Welch**.

I wanted to do other things, and golf takes so much of your time, doesn't it? I was keen on tennis and fishing and I wanted to stay in touch with my friends.—Seventy-five-year-old **Lady Heathcote-Amory**, recalling why she'd played competitive golf for only nine years.

1978

When Nicklaus plays well he wins, when he plays badly he comes second. When he plays terrible, he's third.—**Johnny Miller**.

If a player's ball lies in a mortar shell crater he may move it without penalty.—Notice at Hillside Golf Club, Umtah.

1979

I played so good, it was like the hole kept getting in the way of my ball.—**Calvin Peete**, winner of Milwaukee Open.

If golf were a game of certainties only five men are in it. The only distinction is that they each use different boiler fuels. Nicklaus runs on glory, Trevino on faggots of 100 dollar bills; Player is fired by images of Napoleon, while Irwin and Watson stoke their ambitions with impossible dreams of golfing perfection.—**Peter Dobereiner**.

Mr Noel Staatz, playing in yesterday's open golf championship, was briefly concussed when a seagull dropped a mullet on his head from a height of 300 ft.—*Melbourne Herald*.

I always carry two putters and sometimes I use one just to let the other know I can get along without him.—**Fuzzy Zoeller**.

Roberto de Vicenzo he tell me, don't confuse. He say when you take club from bag just hit ball. Don't think about bunkers or anything. Play with your heart. And 15 times this week at Lytham I am in bunker. Fourteen times I need only one putt after.—**Severiano Ballesteros**.

What is too old? I've been playing on a national basis since 13. If you believe everyone can play and compete for only so long then I'm old. I'm 39 and good gracious! Hogan didn't start playing well till he was 40. Sure, I kid around a lot and say: 'I'm getting too old.' I don't really believe that. If I did I wouldn't say it.—**Jack Nicklaus**.

1980

You cannot love golf any more than you do when you come down the 18th fairway of this golf course a champion.—**Tom Watson**, after winning the British Open for the third time at Muirfield.

If it wasn't for golf, I'd be a caddie today.—**George Archer**, pro golfer.

1981

In the Bob Hope Golf Classic the participation of President Gerald Ford was more than enough to remind you that the nuclear button was at one stage at the disposal of a man who might have either pressed it by mistake or else pressed it deliberately in order to obtain room service.—**Clive James**.

All my life I wanted to play golf like Jack Nicklaus, and now I do.—**Paul Harvey**, ABC commentator, after Nicklaus's 83 at Sandwich.

To improve my golf, I once read one of those great involved books on positive thinking. I gave up when I heard the author had committed suicide.—**Nick Job**.

1982
I owe a lot to my parents, especially my Mum and Dad.—**Greg Norman**.

1983
When you bring stars over and take care of them, it's a hell of a lot of expense. That's what makes the whole thing glamorous.—**Bob Hope**, paid around £200,000 in fees and expenses over four years.

If I could have got the £83,000 owed me by the Bob Hope Classic, I'd still be in business.—**Martin Devetta**, owner of Spandrel Domes.

1985
Winning for me has just been a bonus, especially when for most of my life it has been a guessing game whether I would be able to walk around or not when I woke up.—1984 US Open Champion **Fuzzy Zoeller** after his comeback win at Bay Hill.

1971

To walk from the squash court to the dressing room as weak as a kitten, sweat dripping off you but mind as clear as tomorrow's dawn, is better than five reefers or a trip on LSD.—**John Hopkins.**

It takes more than a war to stop the Indians enjoying their hockey.—**Pat Rowley.**

John Player are getting cut price exposure for a company banned by law for directly advertising its products on TV.—**Ian Wooldridge.**

I am at last beginning to know what dear old Gilbert Harding meant when he described himself as a 'telephoney'.—**Henry Longhurst.**

The competitor in lane four is a real competitor.—**David Coleman.**

1972

I am the greatest single sculler in Argentina. I am the *only* single sculler in Argentina.—**Alberto Demiddi.**

Oh dear, he's laddered his tights.—**Kent Walton**, wrestling commentator.

No one could be utterly dull in the presence of Katharine, Duchess of Kent.—**E. W. Swanton**.

There are no amateurs any more. To be good a skier must literally devote from four to six years of his life to the sport. You don't have time for school or a job, and you must travel the world. That's hard to do without compensation.—**Jean-Claude Killy**.

In four minutes of free skating you're being judged on a whole year of practice. Not many sports put you through that, being the focal point of the entire arena. You've got to look like you're enjoying yourself and accept the judges' decision and not throw a tomato at them. It's tough. —**Peggy Fleming**, a world figure-skating champ at 17, Olympics winner at 19.

My grandfather couldn't prescribe a pill to make a greyhound run faster, but he could produce one to make the other five go slower.—**Benny Green**.

Weightlifting is a sport that gets lost in the suburbs. It is private, obsessive. I'm not at all interested in sport—I *am* interested in obsessions.—**Mai Zetterling** in Munich.

1973

Apart from Neale and Taylor, I can still lick the rest of the England players without any practice—that's how bad the standard is in this country.—**Chester Barnes**.

Mark Cox, the tennis player, pays his gardener more than our top table-tennis players can earn in a week.—**Chester Barnes**.

After a match, whether I win or lose, I never fail to thank God. I need God's help. And if I play with that need I feel at peace. Of course, I must also try. If I close my eyes and say 'God help me' and do nothing myself, that is foolishness.—**Muhammad Lafir**, world billiards champion.

In the old days, at competitions, people would cluster round the champions asking them about their exercise routines. Now they just ask 'What drugs are you on?'—Bodybuilder **Roger Walker**, third in Mr Britain.

Today's radio: 11 a.m. Test Match Special. Hans Keller discusses the influence of Schoenberg on the bowling of Chandrasekhar Ravi-Shankar 4-31.—**Lord Gnome**.

Every sportsman is an egoist.—**Jim Fox**.

We're really going all out not to finish last.—**George Newton**, British weightlifter at world championships.

There's a lot more to getting to the top at judo than running round Regent's Park in thumping great boots.—**Dave Starbrook**.

1974
British sportswriters are the best in the world.—**Harold Wilson**.

If the British working man backs a horse or a dog because of its breeding, why should not the better-bred members of the House of Lords be worthy of our trust in their inherited powers of leadership?—*Daily Telegraph*.

I was a pretty sport until at parties I learned that when you were playing piano there was always a pretty girl standing at the bass-clef end of the instrument. I ain't been no athlete since.—**Duke Ellington**.

A high degree of skill and intelligence are required for croquet and therefore it is not going to attract the lower income groups.—**Croquet Association chairman**, quoted in the *Times*.

I became a woman wrestler 'cos they said I didn't need any O-levels.—**Mitzi Mueller**.

I hope it gets me my Brownies merit badge.—**Samantha White**, aged eight, after becoming the youngest to climb 19,000 ft Mt Kilimanjaro.

Kite flying is as exciting as sex—and Mary Whitehouse can't ban it.—**John Bally**, British champion.

I think caber tossing is absolutely stupid. I feel stupid doing it.—**Arthur Rowe**, Highland Games champion.

Graduate required for coaching to Greek at O-level. N. London area. References essential. Pupil unenthusiastic. Good rowing man would be ideal.
—Advertisement in *Private Eye*.

At squash there is a fantastic and savage and unrivalled and unbelievable satisfaction at the moment you know you have beaten your opponent. There is simply no feeling on earth like it—it is a primitive thing, a conquest, an utter victory. You look into his eyes and you see the defeat there, the degradation, the humiliation, the beaten look and there isn't anything in the world like it.—**Jonah Barrington**.

Cycling is full-pelt, high cross-winds, close formation, all pushing and shoving—it's a real he-man's sport.—**Ian Hallam**.

Be careful, be joyful, be first.—**Mr Korbut**'s advice to daughter Olga.

My ambition is to have a British ski team picked on ability alone, not one that can afford to pay for the honour themselves.—**Robin Bailey**, British Ski Team Manager.

1975

Of the nine judges in the European championships, five came up to me afterwards and said I was the best. They had all placed me fourth. What do you say to that—or to someone who says 'You deserved to win', but then you look up what they gave you and find it was a 5.7. The judging is a pain. It makes you want to spit.—**John Curry**, British skating champion.

Since the age of 14, I have dearly wanted to be regarded as a sex object. I am absolutely sick of being loved for my cooking, accurate seam bowling, ability to solve anagrams, and obtain credit from bookmakers, and yet there are women who profess to be fearful of the alternative.—**Jeffrey Bernard**.

I have always had a secret longing, far stronger than any ambition to be a Cabinet Minister, to walk out to bat in a Test match at Lord's, or still more, to play in one of the later stages on the Centre Court at Wimbledon.—**Robert Carr**, MP.

When Olga Korbut was on, the biggest cheers were coming from the public. But when Tourischeva finished, it was the competitors who were going absolutely mad.—**Pauline Prestige**, national coach.

We're [the International Management Group] by far the most powerful influence on sport in the world. We could turn any individual sport—golf, tennis, skiing—on its ear tomorrow.—**Mark McCormack**, head of International Management Group.

The singing's easy. Memorising the words is hard.—**Rocky Graziano**, making his night club debut.

Sports are the greatest thing that ever happened to TV, the only honest thing that goes on. And I don't just say that because we've got the field surrounded. As the overall quality of TV continues to deteriorate, sports will become even more effective. There's no such thing as too much sport on TV.—**Barry Frank**, vice-president of International Management Group. IMG both manages athletes and packages sports programmes for TV.

The trouble with holidays is, there's plenty of places abroad, but it's finding a place that's big enough to cycle round for three weeks. I mean, Canary Isles is very nice, but it's far too small.—**Beryl Burton**.

1976
Women are to be excluded from the 11th annual conker championships at Oundle. Our event would be ridiculed if women competed.—**Frank Elsom**, chairman of the championship committee.

I am organising an expedition to discover the whereabouts of David Coleman. For some time now the BBC have only been using repeats of his voice. No one can deny David is unique and that our children are being corrupted by the occasional use of five-letter words. If educationists are to gain influence over BBC Sport and allow the use of good English again we will be forced into a literate Minister of Sport.—Letter in *Private Eye*.

Man's obsession with sport can be a real threat to marriage. Not a few homes have been broken on the playing fields of Eton, so much male and female libido is being invested in games.—**Dr J. A. Harrington**, Birmingham medical director.

English country gents often hunt birds and no one objected when Sheikh Zaid Ben Sultan, ruler of Abu Dhabi, decided to try his hand at the sport at his luxurious English mansion in the shires. What distressed neighbours was that he used a machine gun.—*Newsweek*.

The eastern bloc judges didn't mark me down because of either technique or politics. It's just that they don't like champions whom they think are gay.—**John Curry**.

If the law were to abolish blood sports it would create unemployment amongst the working classes.—**Duke of Rutland**.

Maybe now my wife will show more respect.—**Vasily Alexeyev**, on winning the Olympic heavyweight lifting gold medal.

OCCUPATION: Farm worker.—**Franz Klammer's passport entry**.

If you don't like speed, you can't get used to it. It's a nice feeling going at 85 m.p.h., but you also remember what the car looks like when it hits a wall at that speed.—**Franz Klammer**.

1977
Many times on the beach a good looking lady will say to me, 'I want to touch you.' I always smile and say, 'I don't blame you lady.'—**Arnold Schwarzenegger**, Mr Universe.

Remember, postcards only, please. The winner will be the first one opened.—**Brian Moore**.

Sports pages of the popular press are still woefully old-fashioned. Numerous talented sports journalists on popular papers in Fleet Street might as well check in their perceptions, their originality, and their seriousness at the front desk for all the use they'll be allowed to make of them.—**Brian Glanville**.

Look at that tremendous flexibility of the ankles. They really are an extension of the legs.—**Ron Pickering**, gymnastics commentator.

A good darts player who can count can always beat a brilliant player who can't.—**Leighton Rees**, darts champion.

He's going for the pink—and for those of you with black and white sets, the yellow is behind the blue.—**Ted Lowe**, TV snooker commentator.

1978

I play squash twice a week, and jogging round Wimbledon Common is a great joy. One day I sighted three nuns ahead so turned off on to a side path only to run into three people I knew. Also I never miss Match of the Day.—**Cardinal Basil Hume**.

I'm sorry I did not win a gold medal at Prague as expected. This was because (a) I felt exhausted after Edmonton; (b) I was not taking drugs like everyone else; (c) British athletics are so badly organised; (d) I am building up for Moscow '80; (e) I could not live up to my Golden Boy press tag; (f) I had this terrible hangover; (g) I am waiting for the right girl to come along.—**Miles Kington**.

Sir,—The record for the greatest number of symbols added to or removed from the weather map in a single forecast for so long held by that great stalwart, Jack Scott, was broken by Michael Fish in November, 1977. He increased the score from 7 to an unheard of 11 ... but now Bill Giles has scored an unequivocal 14 in the late evening forecast which must surely have ensured his place for the Commonwealth Games.—Letter in the *Guardian*.

Police were searching Eastbourne last night for a middle-aged woman who stabbed Big Bruno Elrington, the 6 ft, 16 stone Portsmouth heavyweight wrestler, who had been thrown out of the ring by his opponent. She thrust a knitting needle into his back before fleeing the hall. Mr Elrington went to hospital for injections.—*The Times*.

Modern players all carry an attache-case with a hair dryer in it. And they've all got headphones. You've got to book three seats on a plane for every two ballplayers so they can put their hi-fis and hair dryers down.—**Cal Griffith**, Minnesota Twins' owner.

This dolphin effect can lead to a sinking situation and might even produce a drowning problem.—**Jim Railton**, BBC, on the Boat Race.

I was vaguely startled to read in a British travel magazine the other day that it would be a good idea 'to explore the unknown parts of Rodney Marsh'. When I re-read the passage, it had changed mysteriously to 'the unknown parts of Romney Marsh'.—**Miles Kington**.

I'm glad to say this is the first Saturday in four weeks that sport will be weather-free.—**David Coleman**.

'I caught them in the act when I flung back the curtains,' said Mrs Juniper Masters, of Carshalton. Denying that he had been adulterous with his dancing partner, Carole Croxley, Mr Robert Masters said: 'I had moved the snooker table into the bedroom for greater elbow room. The noise my wife heard was merely an expression of my delight at having potted the black. The same excitement accounts for the fact that my wig was askew. As for why Miss Croxley had her trousers off—well, she had split the side seam while executing a backhand shot only a few moments before Juniper made her astonishing entry.'—**Christopher Logue**, *Daily Telegraph*.

Not since he once wished viewers a Happy New Year has Frank Bough ever quite said precisely what he means.—**Dennis Potter**.

To put it very simply, spelt out virtually in words of one syllable: Hunt Servants are the salt of the earth. At all times and in all conditions they do their best to provide us with sport. Whether they get a Christmas Box or not, there is no thought of their going on strike.—**Loriner**, *Horse and Hound* columnist.

I went to a fight last night and an ice hockey game broke out.—**Rodney Dangerfield**, comedian.

Talent is overrated. You win with character. In a short series, talent might prevail. Over an 82-game [basketball] season, character prevails.—Former player's agent **Lewis Schaffel**, who moved on to become general manager of the New Orleans Jazz.

Watching the Beeb is something deeper, something occult, something to do with David Coleman's personality. Just by being so madly keen, he helps you get things in proportion. Anything that matters so much to David Coleman, you realise, doesn't matter so much at all.—**Clive James**.

Ron Pickering continued to overheat as usual. The mockery of my confrères had chided him out of saying 'he's pulling out the big one', and even 'he's whacking in the big one'; but the National Viewers' and Listeners' Association will cut off his tail with a carving knife for his new and shameless variant: 'If she hits the board and bangs a big one, that'll put her in the bronze medal position.'—**Julian Barnes**, *New Statesman*.

Stopping otter hunting is unlikely to benefit otters.—*The Field*.

1979
The dictionary definition of a sponsor is 'one who takes responsibility for a paroled delinquent.'—**John Read**, launching Unigate's sponsorship of Real Tennis.

We asked Nadia Comaneci, teasingly, where she'd hidden the smile she throws at the judges. That smile, she explained, had been taught her by her drama coach—part of the act, like the rest of the piled-on cuteness. Determined still to find the little girl in this little girl, we persisted: Can you smile offstage? 'Yes, but I don't care to.' Then do you cry? 'No, I never cry, I have never cried.'—**Brian James**.

You can work out the odds with a pencil and paper. Less than 900 black athletes are earning a living in sports—and not more than 1,500 overall, including coaches and trainers. By comparison, there are perhaps 3 million black youths between [the ages of] 13 and 22 who dream of a career as an athlete. The odds are 20,000 to 1 or worse. Statistically, you have a better chance of getting hit by a meteorite in the next 10 years than getting work as an athlete.—Berkeley (Calif.) sociology professor **Harry Edwards**.

During the 1964 General Election campaign Mr Selwyn Lloyd told me that I should not describe myself as a 'fisherman' but as an 'angler'. There were, he said, 50,000 fishermen with a vote, as against 3,000,000 anglers. —**Lord Home**.

Unquestionably TV is saving sports, although I'm not sure sports is worth saving.—**Howard Cosell**, US TV commentator.

The literature of angling falls into two genres: the instructional and the devotional. The former is written by fishermen who write, the latter by writers who fish.—**William Humphrey**.

The whole crowd is rising to its feet to applaud this man Bryant who is perhaps, without doubt, arguably the greatest bowler of all time.—**Alan Weeks**, BBC.

Stanley Tees, chairman of the Penzance and Zennor sub-aqua club, said: 'Members have been looking forward to diving at Loch Buidhe. Lord Dougall, the owner, gave permission. We drove 700 miles north, climbed 3,000 feet, put on our gear, and then found that the loch is only six inches deep. We were all very depressed.'—*Aberdeen Express*.

A Swiss housewife broke two records when she flew to the Isle of Skye yesterday. She was the first woman to land solo on the island and the first pilot to have an accident on the 2,600-yard Ashaig airstrip.—*The Scotsman*.

During a court of inquiry, Sgt Thomas Green of the SAS admitted he bit Pte Frost's backside while playing 'Murder Ball'. He said: 'The rules are straightforward. A ball is thrown into the air and you have to get it. On the night in question I did bite Frost's buttocks several times. On other occasions I have bitten two captains and a major who were actually on my side. I am regularly bitten myself. Biting is part of the rules, although biting pieces out has been forbidden.'—**Christopher Logue**, *Liverpool Echo*.

1980
Mr Glenn Welt, a computer programmer, has filed a sex discrimination suit against Miami Dolphins, a football cheerleader group. 'I want to be a part of the American tradition of leggy lovelies who cheer their team on. Why deny a person the right to wear panty-hose, leotards and bobbles?' Miss Maytree Lumble, the Dolphins' choreographer, said: 'There is only one thing wrong with Mr Welt—he is an ugly man' (*Daily Telegraph*).
—**Christopher Logue** in *Private Eye*.

The trouble with referees is that they just don't care which side wins.—**Tom Canterbury**, US basketball player.

When I'm thwarted in show business I say to myself it's no worse than a crosscourt drive in squash—and I know how to deal with them.—**Tommy Steele**.

My sport is about 90 per cent strength and 40 per cent technique.—**Johnny Walker**, world middleweight wrist-wrestling champion.

The Government is clutching at sport as a straw with which to beat the Russians.—**Peter Lawson**, ITN.

... and the crowd are absolutely standing up.—**Alan Weeks**, BBC.

He just can't believe what's not happening to
him.—**David Coleman**.

Since squash offers the world's highest energy expenditure
per time allowed of any game, it also offers the world's
greatest sense of exhausted elation in victory and
knackered anguish in defeat.—**Philip Hodson**.

The audience are literally electrified and glued to their
seats.—**Ted Lowe**, BBC.

1981
And that's the third time this session he's missed his
waistcoat pocket with the chalk.—**Ted Lowe**.

Saturday, May 30. Cruise on Windermere with Cyril
Smith. Book Now! Space Limited.'—*Westmorland
Gazette*.

He only needs to be last in this.—**David Vine**, Superstars.

No, I never broke my nose playing ice hockey; but eleven
other guys did.—**Gordie Howe**.

In a pub, worse than the 'buttonholer' is the 'expert'. There's a terribly self-satisfied little jerk in the Coach and Horses—he calls himself an advertising executive, whatever that means—who was telling us all the other day that Botham doesn't hold his bat correctly. He then addressed Mr Botham himself on the television screen and told him to adjust his left hand. He has even given Mr Piggott riding instructions.—**Jeffrey Bernard**.

1982

There is no apartheid practised in South Africa's Grand Prix, because there are no coloured drivers or spectators.—**Mike Reid**.

Admitting he had defrauded her of $10,000, Mrs Suzie Sorensen said: 'On our first date Bennet told me that he was chief beneficiary of a $1M estate, that Paul Newman would be our best man, that his brother was head of the New South Wales mafia, that he had 17 Afghan hounds, and that he had fought Rocky Graziano for the world middleweight title. He seemed very genuine and I fell in love with him inside five minutes.'—*Sydney Morning Herald*.

He didn't intend to miss that one. Ninety-nine times out of a thousand he would have potted it.—**Ted Lowe**.

As for the darts team, it is not true to say there will be no welcome for them—they are valued customers of many years' standing. However, it is true to say that there will be no dart board on the premises after the alterations.—*Stockport Messenger*.

1983
When I took over Jocky (Wilson) in February he was sinking too much vodka and coca-cola. I cut him from 12 to three a night. Now he can hit a playing card side-on.—**Mel Coombes**, darts manager.

1984
We had one netminder who couldn't stop a beachball in a breeze, and one guy who could skate like the wind but never took the puck with him.—**Rod McNair**, Durham Wasps ice hockey coach, on why two North American imports were replaced.

It's embarrassing—we invented the game, but have yet to win the world title.—**Jon Mapley**, unsuccessful British challenger for the Heineken World Championship ... at Tiddlywinks. Larry Khan (US) won 25-17.

I slept like a baby. Every two hours I woke up crying.—**Tom McVie**, coach to New Jersey Devils ice hockey team, on his reaction to disastrous defeat by Buffalo Sabres.

Women are flocking to gyms to train. They're seeing pictures of women athletes on TV—women with no fat, tight bums and firm calves and they say, 'Ah, I like that.'—**Carolyn Cheshire**, body-builder.

I threw a hold and heard the Turk's elbow crack. I thought 'Oh no, they're going to disqualify me'. My brother didn't help when he broke some guy's knee off.—**Mark Schulz,** US wrestling gold medallist. Brother Dave was also in the team.

It was just as if they were a squad of trained paras—every one would die for the other.—**David Whitaker,** British hockey coach after his team's Olympic bronze medal.

I always have to drink six pints before I'm able to start playing properly.—**Bill Werbeniuk,** 20-stone Canadian snooker player who claims to shift 30 pints of lager a day.

Sometimes I feel like a heavyweight boxer coming out of retirement and not really wanting to go through it all again at 35. Snooker is a young man's game now.—**Alex Higgins.**

I was fortunate Steve made so many mistakes—our mother wanted us to tie.—**Phil Mahre,** US special slalom gold medallist, on his twin brother's second place in Sarajevo.

It was like trying to stop a train with a fishing rod.—**Terry O'Dea,** darts player, on being whitewashed in 14 minutes by Jocky Wilson.

I had a bash at positive thinking, yoga, transcendental meditation, even hypnosis. They only screwed me up, so now I'm back to my normal game-plan—a couple of lagers.—**Leighton Rees,** Welsh darts player.

I enjoy sticking it to the Austrians. The Swiss are very nice people, but the Austrians think they should win every time.—**Bill Johnson**, US Olympic downhill champion.

1985

After 13 years I still love basketball—and I'm even starting to enjoy it.—**Jonathan Kovler**, Chicago Bulls vice-president.

I have never skied in Franz Klammer's shadow—I was too good for that.—Swiss downhiller **Peter Mueller** after the Austrian's retirement with five World Cup titles won.

None of us should forget that Klammer put ski racing on the world's television screens.—retired Canadian racer, **Ken Read**.

Karate is like Christianity. Its history has been so riven by disputes between rival sects that sometimes the object of the devotion has been obscured.—**Benjamin Raphael**.

We can alley but we don't have the oop.—**Abe Lemons**, Oklahoma City University basketball coach.

1972

Speed? Really the whole process is the reverse of speed, how to eliminate it. It doesn't exist for me except when I am driving poorly. The things seem to be coming at me quickly instead of passing in slow motion and I know I'm off form.—**Jackie Stewart**.

1973

While the relationship between drivers is superficial, we're the only ones who can talk to each other regarding what we do. We have nobody else to relate to.—**Peter Revson**.

I have always felt I would retire when I stopped enjoying racing, but it occurred to me recently that I may have to find another reason because I may never stop enjoying it.—**Graham Hill**.

As for the accidents and tragedy—the circus goes on. There's no room for tears.—**François Cevert**, a day before he died.

Jackie Stewart faces two options, neither of them very appealing. He can quit racing and save his life, or he can quit racing and lose what his life is about.—**François Cevert**, the day before he died.

1974

Profit isn't a dirty word nowadays. Money is how we keep the score in motor racing nowadays.—**Colin Chapman**.

1975

I'd rather have an accident than fall in love—that's how much I love motor racing.—**Lella Lombardi**, Italian driver.

1976

I hate the bigtime. I feel the loss of close friends terribly. I have to have bouncers at my birthday parties now.—**James Hunt**.

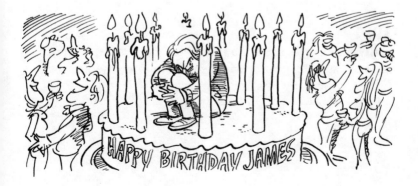

On the day of a big motor race, a lot of people want you to sign something just before you get into your car, just so they can say they got your last autograph.—**A. J. Foyt**.

1977
You just have to treat death like any other part of life.—**Tom Sneva**, US racing driver.

1979
What is called the World Drivers' Championship is in fact the Car Manufacturers' Championship. Drivers are becoming irrelevant.—**James Hunt**.

The battle is well and truly on if it wasn't on before, and it certainly was.—**Murray Walker**, BBC.

1980
Here's Giacomelli, driving like the veteran he is not.
—**Murray Walker**.

... into lap 53, the penultimate last lap but one ...
—**Murray Walker**.

1981
Rally points scoring is 20 points for the fastest, 18 for the second fastest, right down to six points for the slowest fastest.—**Murray Walker**.

1971
One of the factors that is making me prepare for a second Olympics was the death of Lilian Board. She was so young and she never had the chance of a second Games. It made me realise one is lucky to have the opportunity and one must not waste it. It is the story of the parable of the talents.—**David Hemery**.

1972
Goodlooking American gentleman of 50 would like to share tickets for Olympics with nice Bavarian lady, view to also enjoying what translates decorously as happy togetherness.—Advertisement in German press.

I can find no factual evidence that sexual activity in moderation up to and including the night before a match has any detrimental effect. About half an hour of sexual activity, if appropriate, maximises the onset, quantity and quality of sleep.—**Dr Craig Sharp**, consultant to British Olympic canoe squad.

The only time our girls looked good at Munich was in the Village discotheque between nine and eleven every night.—**US coach**.

I still believe in the Olympic idea. Communication between countries is essential; the Games should be a time when the world can step back—two weeks when the people can watch the young and enthuse about health and happiness and joy and peaceful struggles.—**David Hemery**.

The point I'm reaching for in my little crusade is to modernise a code that goes back to the Gay '90s. ... The British aristocracy had set it up to keep those of a lower social level from competing against them. But sport is no longer the dilettante thing it once was, a casual hour-a-day thing. It's an all-out approach that practically demands cheating.—**John B. Kelly, Jr**, Association of American Universities president, claiming that the Olympics amateur code was leading to perjury among Olympic athletes.

1975
If only politicians had to sweat it out to get to the Olympics they might not be quite so keen to say to we sportspeople, 'Sorry, you're not going'.—**Princess Anne**.

It is not a question of dictating to Europe. If people in Britain can sit at home, and get 60 hours of TV Olympics for 20 cents—well, tell me any theatre or cinema that gives such value.—**Roger Rousseau**, Montreal Commissioner-General.

1976
The 33 cranes rented by Montreal to complete building the Olympic site cost £1 million more than it would have been to buy them.—*Montreal Star*.

There's one way I can get maximum security cover for the Olympics. But everyone must stay home first.—**General Roland Reid**, Montreal military co-ordinator.

It's easier to win the Olympics than the US championships. At the Olympics you only have three Americans to beat.—**Guy Drut**, French Olympic hurdling champion.

There's Parnham of Britain in last position. I'm afraid the conditions are so calm that they don't suit Doug Parnham; he's always at his best paddling into a headwind.—**John Motson** at Olympic canoeing.

1978

Many athletes have told me that steroids very likely do have a positive effect on them. Is that positive effect because they are training and thus motivated, or does it really put on a lot of bulk and thereby make them stronger? That's what we've got to find out. I've yet to meet an Olympic or world-class weight lifter who hasn't felt it has been beneficial to his performance. Athletes would like not to take steroids. They don't feel good or right about it, but they're afraid not to, because they're concerned about what the next athlete might be doing.—**Dr Irving Dardik**, chairman of the US Olympic Sports Medicine Commission.

1980

Michelle Ford is Australia's first gold medallist for four years.—**Norman May**, ABC Radio.

At a meeting of the North Sotby Olympics Committee, Mr John Fawcett suggested that the Games should take place in Moscow as agreed, but that the Russians should not be allowed to take part.—*Lincolnshire Echo*.

1983

Let's be honest—a proper definition of an amateur today is one who accepts cash, not cheques.—**Jack Kelly Jr**, US Olympic Committee.

1984

I do think even housing benefits are put into perspective on occasions like this.—**Rhodes Boyson** MP, winding up a Commons debate after news of Torvill and Dean's gold in the Sarajevo Winter Olympics.

I'm looking forward to gloating over the performances of the US athletes.—**Larry Ellis**, US men's coach, before the LA Olympics.

Ladies and gentlemen, would you please rise for the playing of the national anthem of the United States of America.—Announcement made 80 times at Olympics.

The boycotts are not so terrible. There's no death involved. Olympics have survived massacres, cataclysms, destruction and 16 centuries of slumber; they are stronger than boycotts.—**Monique Berlioux**, IOC Director.

The Chinese are much more intellectual in their sport than the East Germans and much more up-to-date than the Dr Arnold people.—**Lord Killanin** at the LA Olympics.

As long as an American is standing after three rounds, it's hard to get a decision.—**Redzep Redzepovski**, Yugoslav boxer and silver medallist.

Reporter: What did Princess Anne say to you after you'd won, and who's going to be the mother of your kids?
Daley Thompson: Well, you've just mentioned the lady. And the answer to the first question is, she said 'I hope they'll be white'.—Press conference exchange after Thompson's decathlon victory.

It would be wonderful to be so pretty.—**Zola Budd** on her idol, Decker, in San Diego pre-Olympics.

Don't bother.—**Mary Decker** to Budd when the South African girl went to enquire about her health after the race.

When you're behind, you're the one to have to watch out. It was Mary's fault.—**Cornelia Burki**, fifth in the Budd–Decker race.

I'm tired of seeing my name in the same paragraph with Zola Budd.—**Mary Decker** before their Olympic clash.

What joy it has been to drive down streets and see American flags flying. ... The young athletes of the world have performed a miracle—they've brought back patriotism. Bless them all.—Letter to *LA Times*, August.

The Olympics make too many people very nationalistic. All that talk of brotherhood. Why, we've known our competitors for years, meeting them in other tournaments. And the anger and the spite you saw in our game today—it's hard to square that with the ideals.—**Richard Charlesworth**, Australian hockey and Labor MP, in LA.

In a country like the US, beauty is emphasised. Superficial beauty, make-up. In the Eastern bloc it's just not a necessity for women to look like Mary Decker, who looks like she goes two hours before the meet and puts on make-up and curls her hair.—**Ria Stalman**, Dutch discus gold medallist.

I don't have a Daley Thompson complex. Someday I'll beat him, I'm sure. Of course, I may be 80 by then.—**Jurgen Hingsen**.

If the Russians had done half in Moscow what the Americans did in LA everyone would have screamed. In Moscow it was pretty fair play, the Americans were not fair play at all.—**Monique Berlioux**, IOC director.

The best moment since I caught my tit in a mangle.—**Daley Thompson** on his gold medal.

If someone is good looking and a medal winner, the combination is virtually unbeatable. Then there are those who are very attractive but were also-rans. They still have a chance of making money.—**Nina Blanchard**, head of agency arranging commercial endorsements for athletes after Olympics.

1971

I know a bit more about form than I did in my army days.—**Lord Wigg.**

There are, they say, fools, bloody fools, and men who remount in a steeplechase.—**John Oaksey.**

1972

If another jockey asks you for a bit of room at a fence, you bloody well give it. Next time you might be asking him. There's quite enough trouble out there without making any of our own.—**Terry Biddlecombe.**

When a horse hits a fence his speed decelerates in a split second while the jockey's body goes straight on. Overcoming this distressing tendency is one of the skills a rider had better acquire if he wants to stay in the business.—**John Oaksey.**

The men who run racing reflect the picture of the country as I see it—a group of political, social and economical mules. I wouldn't normally expect to mix with them, nor they me.—**Lord Wigg.**

Racing is like politics—it's full of good rogues.—**Eddie Harty**.

Brigadier Gerard did not win the Derby because he did not run in it. He did not run in it because he was not bred for it. He wasn't bred for it because I couldn't afford it.—Owner **John Hislop**.

It's a lot tougher to get up in the mornings when you start wearing silk pyjamas.—Former jockey **Eddie Arcaro**, who won 4,779 races and $30 million in purses over two decades.

1973

The Queen Mother always rings me after any of her horses have run and says: 'How are my darlings?'—**Jack O'Donoghue**, one of her trainers.

Up in the press box at the Grand National are all the racing journalists, back to the field, straining to get a peek at the TV set to see what's happening.—**Stanley Reynolds**.

Morston for the Derby.—**Richard Baerlein**.

In all the years that I have known the Queen Mother she has never asked me or any of her friends to place a bet for her on one of her horses.—**Sir Martin Gilliat**, Private Secretary.

Short odds and betting tax have put the professional punter out of business. The rest of the betting public only accept the odds because they don't realise what's happening. Odds are so short today that you just can't get on some horses.—**Richard Baerlein**.

Jockeys are only really there to win on the ones that aren't meant to win.—**Terry Biddlecombe**.

If you lose a race it's a matter of passing the buck: the owner blames the trainer, the trainer blames the jockey, the jockey blames the poor old horse.—**Tony Murray**.

1974

A chronic gambler who says he backed a winning horse every time he prayed in church for help to clear his debts was so impressed by the power of prayer that he has become a Catholic priest.—*Daily Telegraph* report.

Don't bother with Ascot unless you remember to raise your topper to the Queen's representative, the Marquis of Abergavenny (pronounce it Ab-venny), and to totally remove your hat if a member of the Royal Family happens to pass by. But don't cheer please.—**Paul Callan**.

Things have become so serious that unless immediate action is taken the racing industry as we know it will be gone inside two years.—**Richard Baerlein**.

Since I've been on the telly every night my life's not been my own. I can't even put a bet on in a betting shop in peace nowadays.—**Joe Gormley**.

The small betting-shop punter may have fun, but he can't possibly win. No chance.—**John Banks**.

There will never be another like Lester—and I don't think there ever has been one like him.—**Pat Eddery**.

1975
Lester rarely says anything to anyone unless it's asking you about horses. But he never asks me because he knows I won't tell him. But the only way some jockeys can get anywhere to him is by telling him about what such-and-such a horse is like to ride. They're mad. I won't tell him anything. No way. Because for sure he'd pinch it.—**Pat Eddery**.

I'm personally holding out for less than I'm getting.
—**Striking Newmarket stable lad**.

In an attempt to glamorise a dying industry, the sports dictionary has been turned upside down: centre forwards are strikers, throw-ins are set pieces, the pitch is now the park. In racing, grooms are calling themselves trainers, and when a horse is referred to as an in-and-out performer, it means it only wins when the stable has backed it. And a racing correspondent is now a would-be gentleman without a private income.—**Jeffrey Bernard**.

1976
The reason I like those high-class Englishmen is that they sure appreciate a good horse.—**Bunker Hunt**.

1977
A jump jockey's got to throw his heart over the fence—and then get over and catch it.—**Dick Francis**.

The trainer, Jeremy Tree, quizzed Lester Piggott hard one day. 'I've got to speak to the boys of my old school, Lester, and tell them all I know about racing. What shall I say?' The jockey paused and then gave a short, muffled reply: 'Tell 'em you've got flu.'—**Tony Lewis**.

He had always been a man to bear misfortune with stoical endurance. A racehorse owner for the past 20 years, he had his first winner—Goblin—only three weeks ago.
—*Sunday Telegraph*.

One day I had breakfast with the Queen. She was fantastic to talk racing with, but I was even more nervous than when I rode in the Oaks. We had scrambled eggs and tea. 'I do like tea to be tea,' she said, which means she likes it to be strong.—**Willie Carson**.

1978

Getting Steve Cauthen to ride your horse with a five-pound allowance is like having a license to steal, and trainers know it. Cauthen looks like the best young rider to come onto the race track since Willie Shoemaker in 1949.—Former jockey **Sammy Renick**, on the 16-year-old apprentice jockey, winner of 29 races and $375,000 in purses in his first 21 days of racing in New York.

It's one thing to ask your bank manager for an overdraft to buy 500 begonias for the borders in Haslemere, but quite another to seek financial succour to avail oneself of some of the 5-2 they're offering on Isle de Bourbon for the St Leger.—**Jeffrey Bernard**.

I was unable to collect my £91,000 ITV Seven winnings from the bookmaker because I couldn't find the time. I was so busy on the allotment, and also had to feed my chickens, that I couldn't fit it in.—**Frank Bradley**, assistant seedsman.

At Ascot today the heat is quite hot.—**Judith Chalmers**.

1979

I still ride out twice a week, but I do tend to get a couple of boils on my bottom nowadays.—**Sir Gordon Richards**.

Nonsense, the rule about divorcees not being allowed into the Royal Enclosure at Ascot was abolished years ago. And even then it only referred to guilty parties. You have always been allowed in if you were innocent.—**Anne Ainscough**, St James's Palace Ascot office.

England is small, it's beautiful, and the whole little place is just horse crazy.—**Steve Cauthen**.

The Jockey Club have always had their priorities wrong. Their number one priority is the future of the Jockey Club. Their number two priority is the future of racing.—**Richard Baerlein**.

1981

And there's the unmistakable figure of Joe Mercer—er, or is it Lester Piggott?—**Brough Scott**.

1985

I arrived at Aintree without a care in the world because I thought we had no chance.—**Tim Forster**, trainer of the Grand National winner, Last Suspect.

1974

We are breeding a nation of pansies.—**Albert Fearnley**,
Bradford rugby league manager.

1978

Ted Dexter is to journalism what Danny La Rue is to
Rugby League.—**Michael Parkinson**.

Let's see again where that move started ... there you are,
see, it started from its origins.—**Eddie Waring**, BBC.

1983

I want to sell Rugby League to the local people. The
match ball for our first game will be brought to the pitch by
parachute. We also plan to have majorettes and Morris
dancers. After all, this is Kent.—**Paul Faires**, Kent
Invicta's first chairman.

The conditions were very hot. I asked one of the lads after
the match how he felt—I won't tell you what he said but it
begins with N.—**Alex Murphy** on Radio Manchester after
Salford–Wigan game.

My wife doesn't want me to walk through the town and have people pointing and saying, 'That's him. He's *sine die*. Dirty Dalgreen'. I'm not really dirty, I'm very kind and generous. I'm very quiet off the field, a family man. I don't drink very much and I don't smoke. I like to potter around the home. I'm not a ruffian, I'm really not.—**John Dalgreen**, Fulham RL hooker, on his life ban, later lifted.

1984

The neighbours, in their £80,000 terraced houses, who caused so much disruption at first, can go back to enjoying their Sunday afternoons in peace.—**Brian Dalton**, Fulham Rugby League director, announcing original club's closure.

We've paid an awful lot of money for three bags of kit and a few balls.—**Barbara Close**, chairman of Fulham RL club, after the High Court declared players free agents.

On Mondays, which I set aside for developing skills and positional play, there were sometimes only four or five players turning up. From the others I'd get excuses like 'My wife was having a Tupperware party'.—**Geoff Wraith**, on his resignation as Wakefield Trinity coach.

I wouldn't play the French at marbles, never mind Rugby League. All we will ever learn off them is how to fight and spit and bite each other.—**Alex Murphy**, ex-Wigan coach.

1971
Rugby is not all that important to me. I just play for the fun of it. It's not the most vital thing in life, is it?—**Barry John**.

Sunday Game: USA v. Rest of the World. Loser Buys Beer.—Extract from newsletter of Manhattan RFC, New York.

1972
My mother was up there in the stand. She doesn't know a bugger about rugby, but she knows we won.—**Delme Thomas**, Llanelli's captain.

I've never taken anything on tour but grey slacks and the All Black blazer. It's all you've got to wear, it's all you *want* to wear.—**Ian Kirkpatrick**.

1973

I was able to stay in my natural environment and develop there and become a respected member of the community. But if I was taken as a 15-year-old from Belfast and pitched into Old Trafford I really feel I would have reacted just as George has. I could not have stood it.—**Barry John**.

Now I look at it all out there on the field and think, crikey, was I ever in the middle of that lot?—**Barry John**.

Rugby people, who I knew to be kind thoughtful Socialists still wrap the cloak of the game around themselves when it comes to touring South Africa.—**John Morgan**.

1974

I don't know why prop forwards bother to play rugby.—**Lionel Weston**.

Any Rugby Union player worth his salt in France who does not accept payment is considered a fool and a rare one at that.—**Chris Laidlaw**.

Welsh supporters are one-eyed and Welsh players are cheats.—**Sid Going**.

Rugby is fun. Athletics hurts.—**Andy Ripley**.

When John Williams, the Welsh full-back, took up rugby, he quite simply revolutionised the whole game.—**Andy Irvine**.

Multi-racial sport—or isolation. That seems the logical choice for South Africa.—**Carwyn James**.

The French selectors never do things by halves: for the first International of the season against Ireland they had dropped half their threequarter line.—**Nigel Starmer-Smith**.

When Willie John speaks, you realise you are listening to a legend.—**Dick Milliken**, Lion.

1975

I am not satisfied unless I am completely dictating to my opposite prop. Some people threaten me. I would rather just hit someone. I don't say things like 'That's your last warning'. I just hit him and tell him that's the first warning. Then I would hit him again and keep doing it until he has stopped messing me about.—**Ian McLauchlan**.

Rugby players are either piano shifters or piano players. Fortunately I'm one of those who can play a tune.—**Pierre Danos**, French player.

1976

No world-class backs have emerged in Britain since J. P. R. Williams and David Duckham in 1969. Never before this century have we gone anything like seven years without producing one player good enough to rank alongside the greatest in our heritage.—**John Reason**.

I'm the only man I reckon who's trained with the England rugby team in jeans. No time for fancy tracksuits. I suppose I don't suffer from cold legs like some I could mention.—**Stack Stevens**.

How to pick a good English forward at rugby? Simply look for someone who is working his guts out in the last 20 minutes on a wet Wednesday night in an away match at Aberavon.—**Dave Rollitt**.

Sir,—I suggest that on the next occasion England play at Twickenham the following words be sung to the tune of the National Anthem: 'God Bless St George's Land / Mighty of Heart and Hand / England's The Land We Love / Let's Give a Mighty Shove / God Save Our Land.' Inspired by this and with more practice at passing and kicking, England could well start winning.—Letter in *Rugby World*.

Imaginative English rugby seems to have vanished. Let us have backs who can run. There is far too much talk of good ball and bad ball—in my opinion good ball is when you have possession and bad ball is when the opposition have it.—**Dick Jeeps**, RFU president.

1977

Nigel Starmer-Smith had seven craps for England some years ago.—**Jimmy Hill**.

The Lions make a great pack—of animals. The touring rugby side is a disgrace to its members and their homeland. There has been only one word to describe their behaviour here—disgusting! Two have urinated down stairwells, others have ripped seven hotel doors off their hinges. In another town Lions have thrown glasses, turned over tables, uncoiled water hoses and sprayed water.—*New Zealand Truth*.

1979

When he was rugby football correspondent of *The Times* the late U. A. Titley declined to use the first names of players in his reports since in most cases he had not been introduced to them.—**Geoffrey Nicholson**.

No longer are the rules by which he kicks a football a reflection on a child's social or professional aspirations. Boys at school are allowed to be boys—to play, for the fun of it, any game they fancy. Marvellous! Until they reach the age of 18. Then the Rugby Union authorities drive in a brutal wedge.—**Colin Welland**.

Goddammit! The buggers have blown it again!—**England rugby supporter** after All Black's match.

Mr R. F. Cunningham, industrial relations section, personnel department, Head Office, to the roar of an 80,000 capacity crowd, ran on to the pitch at Murrayfield last month ready and eager to get to grips with the New Zealand 'All Blacks' in the last international of their recent British tour.—*Hydro News*.

1980

In last month's issue the replacement of the word 'objectives' by 'objections' made it seem that John Lawrence of the Rugby Union was agreeing wholeheartedly with Peter Hain about the South African tour.—Apology in *Rugby World*.

West Wales breed the fly-halves, the Gwent valleys produce the mighty forwards.—**Carwyn James**.

The coloured kids are sad and aware that the Lions being here means Britain has forsaken them. When I watch the Lions on television my two teenage sons, who love sport, get up and go quietly to their room and play sad music.—**Hassan Howa**.

1982

When I complete my studies I hope to specialise in sports injuries. That will be my way of putting something back into rugby in return for what I have received from it.—**Ivan Serfontein**, *Johannesburg Sunday Times*.

1983

The main difference between League and Union is that now I get my hangovers on Mondays instead of Sundays.—**Tommy David**, Cardiff City prop.

I want a team capable of playing positive attacking rugby, and that's why this team has been chosen.—**Jim Telfer**, Lions' coach, before tour to New Zealand.

Rugby can be a very violent game if there is £1,000 a man riding on the result.—**Bob Weighill**, RFU secretary, on the proposed professional circus.

The biggest hindrance is that we don't appear to know what we are doing in Britain and Ireland. If we're to continue touring New Zealand as the Lions every six years, you can't bring out players who take so long to adjust—and some never do.—**Jim Telfer** after the tour, in which the Lions lost all four Tests.

On the club circuit in England and Wales, there are roughly a dozen players whom I'd describe as psychopathic thugs. I don't think that's going over the top. In the context of what happened to me, that description is not too strong.—**John Davidson**, Moseley RU prop, forced to retire after his jaw and cheekbone were fractured by a Swansea player.

1984

If Wales went to war with Russia tomorrow, I honestly reckon Wales would have a bloody good chance.—**Andrew Slack**, Wallabies' captain before Wales game.

No leadership, no ideas. Not even enough imagination to thump someone in the line-out when the ref wasn't looking.—**J. P. R. Williams** after the Wallabies defeated Wales.

I don't enjoy the way British teams play. When I came here three years ago, everyone was trying to win games by kicking rather than scoring tries. Things haven't changed.—**Mark Ella**, Wallabies fly-half.

I take the Gucci view about hard work on the practice field—long after you've forgotten the price, the quality remains.—**Alan Jones**, Australian RU coach, on completing Grand Slam.

No letter, no explanation, no rule-book thrown at me.—**Ray French**, Rugby League TV commentator, on his suspension from coaching Rugby Union in Lancashire schools.

I played 10 injury-free years between the ages of 12 and 22. Then suddenly it seemed I was allergic to the 20th century.—**Nigel Melville**, England Rugby Union captain.

The knee doesn't trouble me when I'm walking, but it's painful when I kneel, like before my bank manager.—**David Leslie**, Scottish RU International.

Reporter: What of the future for Welsh rugby?
Mike Watkins (Welsh captain): Over to the Angel for a lot of pints.—Exchange after Wales v. Australia game.

1985

As coach I'll always pick a team rather than a goalkicker.—**Mick Doyle**, after Ireland's Triple Crown success.

1972

I've never liked sailing men. They yell blue murder at you all day, but then, when the boat is moored, the whisky comes out, Captain Bligh turns Casanova and is all ready to seek out your jolly erogenous zones, and play deck coitus.—**Jilly Cooper.**

Winning is easy. It's far harder, once you've won, to lose honourably. I suppose I'll be beaten eventually. I only hope I accept it graciously.—**Rodney Pattison.**

1974

I turned to God at sea: I prayed every day. Never on land. You know how insignificant you are at sea; on land it seems to matter that you change your car each year.—**Chay Blyth.**

1975

I run a dry boat. And over a two-day race we eat only apples or Mars. If I gave the crew even fresh-made sandwiches they'd 'protect' them in trouble. With apples or Mars, they're happy to drop them at once and start pulling ropes.—**Edward Heath MP.**

I enjoy helming more than anything. I don't get any fun at all out of winching.—**Edward Heath MP**.

1977

If I only had a little humility, I would be perfect.—Yachtsman **Ted Turner**, after winning the America's Cup.

Lone yachtsman Prasantha Mukherjee was saved from the sea by British soldiers ten minutes after he sailed from Hamble to Calcutta yesterday. 'I was carrying several large sacks of curry powder and a generous quantity of Quaker Oats and lentils,' he explained, as he left hospital. 'My boat was designed for racing and the provisions weighed her down.' The rescue operation cost £80,000. 'It is our job to save human life,' said an Army spokesman.—*Evening Express*.

1984

They [the New York Yacht Club] were afraid of us; they tried not to race us, and we proved they were right.—**Alan Bond**.

1971

Banksie doesn't know how lucky he was! He bloody near got kissed on the lips in front of 40,000!—**John Ritchie** of Stoke City, after Banks had saved Hurst's penalty in the League Cup semifinal.

Queen in rumpus at Palace.—*Guardian* headline.

I realised Gordon knew where I put my penalties.—**Geoff Hurst**.

I recently bought three books by Russia's Nobel prize-winner, Alexander Solzhenitsyn.—**George Best**.

There is narcissism in every referee. I honestly believe that a great many referees around the world have effeminate tendencies.—**Joao Saldanha**, former Brazilian soccer manager.

In modern society one earns what one is worth.—Italian soccer coach **Helenio Herrera**, responding to the criticism that his $240,000 salary was ten times that of a government minister.

Don't expect too many miracles before Christmas.—**Don Howe**, on taking over as West Bromwich Albion's manager.

What is it, being a footballer? If you take away Match of the Day and the Press and the fans and the hangers-on, it's all very empty and lonely.—**Rodney Marsh**.

Because football is so badly reported a great number of spectators are ignorant about the game. One solution might be to cut down on the free drink provided in the Press box.—**Patrick Marnham**.

The Greek squad to face Neasden in the second leg of the Inter-Suburbs European Nations Cup was named in Athens yesterday. It reads: Xenophon, Egganchippolatas, Aristophones, Menopaus, Owatalotigotides, Kikiminthebolox, Logarithm, Thycydides, Chrystalpallas, Delicatessen, Underneathearchas.—**Lord Gnome**.

Every team has a clogger whose job it is to put a clever opponent out of the match.—**Harry Catterick**, manager of Everton.

I wouldn't want to be a referee under the present system because I'd need the IQ of a super university professor.—**Alan Hardaker**.

The ref could not speak a word of English, but he spoke German all right. Overath spent the whole match chatting him up.—**Frank McLintock**.

Of course a player can have sexual intercourse before a match and play a blinder. But if he did it for six months he'd be a decrepit old man. It takes away the strength from the body.—**Bill Shankly**, manager of Liverpool.

The crowds tell me to go home or catch a banana boat. I just laugh. With Charlie George it's his long hair. With me it's my colour.—**Brendon Batson**, Grenada-born Arsenal reserve.

1972

What they say about footballers being ignorant is rubbish. I spoke to a couple yesterday and they are quite intelligent.—**Raquel Welch**.

I did not enjoy 'The Godfather' at all.—**Bobby Moore**.

I'm not a naturally modest bloke.—**Charlie George**.

We were going to Portugal for our holiday, but now it looks like Bermuda—that may be just far enough away to steer clear of George Best and all his problems.—**Bobby Charlton**.

Ex-United players are meant to have wings on their feet or something.—**Francis Burns**.

If I died tomorrow, I'd be quite happy. Even being barracked at Fulham was a pleasure, though I didn't think so at the time.—**Jimmy Hill**.

In Seville, peeping through an irongrilled casement, but inside no Barber, only two nuns glued to a quacking television set showing 'Match of the Day'.—**Philip Hope-Wallace**.

If they knee me I butt 'em.—**Charlie George**.

Pele couldn't get into my squad the way my lads are playing these days.—**Pat Saward**, Brighton manager.

No team has worked harder than the winners of that match—or indeed the losers.—**Barry Davies**, BBC commentator.

1973
I don't drop players. I make changes.—**Bill Shankly**.

Pity I didn't get my eyebrows on telly sooner; really you can cop a lot of easy loot in this panel lark, can't you.—**Terry Venables**.

I know exactly how George Best feels. If I were him I'd be running away every week.—**David Bedford**.

I thought the England team played magnificent.—**Sir Alf Ramsey**.

English soccer is based on force. Most teams in the World Cup have force too, but they also have flair.—**Ferrucio Valcareggi**, Italy's team manager.

English football has degenerated to unbelievable levels. The hackers are now completely in charge.—**Johnny Byrne**.

If it is possible to make a million out of soccer, I would like to be the first to do it.—**Bobby Moore**.

Football is business, and business is business.—**Rinus Michels**, Barcelona coach.

Those who tell you it's tough at the top have never been at the bottom.—**Joe Harvey**.

The great failing of modern football is the amount of inter-passing without gain.—**Walter Winterbottom**.

There's no fun in soccer any more. It's all deadly serious. We'll end up playing in cemeteries.—**Terry Venables**.

I don't care about politics. The impact of soccer is much healthier and deeper than politics.—**Johann Cruyff**.

The day I pack it in I'll have an almighty sense of relief.—**Steve Heighway**.

I'm very placid most of the time, but I blow up very quickly. I shout and I wave my arms, my lip twitches, I become incoherent, and I swear. All at the same time.—**Jack Charlton**.

Any British side that tries to beat Lazio at their own game soon discover that the Italians have a big advantage in terms of match practice.—**Hugh McIlvanney**.

Matches are won and lost between Monday and Friday—not on Saturday afternoons.—**Peter Taylor**, Clough's No. 2 at Brighton.

Strikers today don't seem to need any stitches. Forty times my face was cut so badly it needed stitching. And they say it's harder now.—**John Charles**.

St Anthony, Blessed Oliver Plunkett and St Theresa: Many thanks for finding lost UEFA Cup ticket.—Ad in *Liverpool Echo*.

I may not make myself popular saying it, but the decline of cricket as a character builder has had a lot to do with our present situation. As soon as soccer became the so-called national sport, the whole idea of a game that was played for its own sake among people who understood each other went by the board.—**Frederick Raphael**.

The Game has lost some of its beauty in gaining speed. Today the rhythm is like rock; it used to be like the tango.—**Francesco Grosso**, Juventus coach.

Footballers' wives should be seen and not heard.—**Tony Waiters**.

Few teams in the history of football can have leapt to fame as rapidly as Sunderland. The Club was founded in 1879.—*FA Year Book 1973–74*.

The irony is that if Sir Alf felt obliged to quit he might well be leaving the best side he has ever had.—**Jimmy Hill**.

I remember when I was sent off against Chelsea. They flashed my picture up on the TV screen that night—and it made me a hero at home. We'd come from nothing and here I was on TV.—**Derek Jefferson**, Wolves.

There's a tradition in football that full backs always cart a winger early on. To teach him, I stopped waiting for that to happen, and started going looking for them. They all know by now it's no use thumping me because I'm going to thump right back. Eighty per cent of defenders have got hearts like peanuts—so used to dishing it out they've never learned to take it.—**Mike Summerbee**.

The World Cup without England will be like a wedding without the bride, a party without champagne.—Editorial in Cologne newspaper.

Some people think football is a matter of life and death. I don't like that attitude. I can assure them it is much more serious than that.—**Bill Shankly**.

If West Ham's soccer is unhealthy, then English soccer is unhealthy.—**Joe Mercer**.

Tommy Finney was grisly strong. If he was about now I could play him in his overcoat and there would be four men marking him when we were shooting in.—**Bill Shankly**.

Whaddya mean giving one of my players orange juice? I'm not having him spoiling his beauty sleep by having to get up in the night for a pee.—**Bill Shankly**.

Palace's psychiatrist tells us that people who are friends pass more to each other.—**Malcolm Allison**.

It's tight, taut, and muscular. Bobby Moore's posterior comes top of our Girls' Bottom League.—*The Sun*.

A pub called the 'Sir Alf Ramsey' will attract all the wrong sort of persons.—**Tunbridge Wells resident**.

I go, I come back.—**George Best**.

Of course we are going to continue playing in Europe. How else can we all get duty-free cigarettes.—**John Cobbold**, Ipswich chairman.

Which side went out to retaliate first?—**Danny Blanchflower**.

Why didn't they tell us that England's centre-forward was in fact a Polish agent called Shivas.—**Clive James**.

With Jimmy Hill a little humility would work wonders.—**Brian Glanville**.

Soccer is run by second-rate con-men. Petit-bourgeois, frustrated small businessmen. It's a tragedy because, socially, football is very important.—**Eamonn Dunphy**.

What's wrong with the game? Too many David Colemans, who know it all, for a start. And too many pooftas, flash types. 'It's the in thing, duckey.' They don't know Alan Ball from Charlie George yet they prance around here after leaving their flash cars, Jensens and that, over in Finsbury Park or Green Lanes, so they won't get damaged by us nasty lads. Well, one of these days, they're in for a shock.—**Frank Rowe**, 17, Arsenal supporter.

1974

The quiet of the church was shattered by rhythmic clapping and the shouting of 'England' as Rev. Stevens spoke of the patriotism of St George being manifested in the cry for England's football team.—*Twickenham Times*.

It was always football for me—when girls at school passed me love letters under the desk, I flicked them back. I never squeezed the spots on my face 'cos I wanted to be repulsive and keep the girls away.—**Alan Ball**.

Football is about playing: if you don't turn up at 3 p.m., that's it. A lot of bullshit is being talked about football and Pop: Dylan doesn't have to give concerts week in week out. Footballers can record their skills on plastic. Elvis didn't have to come to England to be Elvis—but Best had to go to Old Trafford to be Best.—**Steve Grant**.

Deaf viewers are to protest about the language by players on 'Match of the Day'. Although most viewers could not distinguish the words, the country's deaf lip-read the exchange.—*Daily Telegraph* report.

I had never admired a man as much as Matt Busby. But when I left Old Trafford I had never been let down by any man as much as by him.—**Frank O'Farrell**.

No European gentleman would act like Mr Havelange has.—**Sir Stanley Rous**.

Footballers now know money business better than football business.—**Joao Saldanha**.

It was the sort of football that would bring the crowds in any Saturday of the week.—**Wally Barnes** on West Ham v. Wolves.

I know more about football than politics.—**Harold Wilson**.

The only word never used to describe what happens in football is 'kick'. The ball is always 'volleyed' or 'struck' or 'driven'. 'Kick' only happens when players do it to each other.—**Penelope Gilliatt**.

I am expecting a call from Tottenham—and there again I am not expecting one, if you see what I mean.—**Danny Blanchflower**.

The Lynn and West Norfolk FA Commission are still making inquiries about the abandoned Upwell Res. v. Southery A match because the game was resumed with a completely different referee and with the same player who had been sent off by the first referee.—*East Anglian Times*.

I have an instinct to do the wrong things. That's probably my secret.—**Johann Cruyff**.

Of course I'm against Sunday soccer. It'll spoil my Saturday nights.—**John Ritchie**, Stoke City.

This trip is a bloody shambles; the jokers, the jet-set are running his squad. You see things happening in the hotel or at training that make you want to puke. The boss is a great wee man, but he's not strong enough.—**Scottish World Cup player**.

What has happened to Crystal Palace is like watching your child take drugs.—**Arthur Wait**, former chairman.

If Stan Bowles could pass a betting shop like he can pass a ball he'd have no worries at all.—**Ernie Tagg**, his manager at Crewe.

When the full story of Manchester United in recent years is told Sir Matt Busby will not be its hero.—**J. L. Manning**.

Three-up, three-down is ludicrous: managers are asked only two things after each game now—'will you avoid relegation, and if so, will you get into Europe?'—**Tony Waddington**.

How much further down his head will Bobby Charlton have to part his hair before he faces the fact that he is bald.—**Clive James**.

Glasgow's violence and Scotland's shame is a surfeit of bad sex. If Scotland's football hooligans had it off before they reached the terraces they'd be less likely to reach for the nearest sharp object to stick in the opposition. —**Gordon McGill**.

I'd like to see a return of the wingers, the days of Matthews and Finney, Hancocks and Mullen, Huntley and Palmer, Fortnum and Mason. —**Eric Morecambe**.

Our decline as a football power started when boot styles changed and the wogs no longer knew what it was like to be on the receiving end of a British toecap. —**Michael Parkinson**.

The cult of the manager is ridiculous and embarrassing: I've had standing ovations on some grounds while the players themselves don't warrant a cheep. —**Jack Charlton**.

I love Liverpool so much that if I caught one of their players in bed with my missus I'd tiptoe downstairs to make him a cuppa tea. —**Koppite**.

I have seen myself described as an ash-faced hard man or, as it has been put, 'iron' man. I don't think this opinion is necessarily correct: I would say that I think, quite categorically, that I am a gentleman. —**Ronald Saunders**, Aston Villa manager.

If a soccer hooligan is brought before the magistrates for a second time the label 'FA THUG' should be branded for life on his forehead. —Letter in *Portsmouth Evening News*.

... and the crowd are encouraging referee Thomas to blow his watch.—**Hugh Johns**, ITV commentator.

Although some footballers are in the super-tax class, it is worth pointing out that they are still, according to the Registrar-General's classification of occupations, listed in Class 4 alongside bank detectives, butlers, furriers, market gardeners, publicans and toy designers.—**Maurice Yaffe**.

1975

At Burnley, no moustaches, no sideburns, long hair discouraged ... and four kids of 18 suspended for being caught having a drink on Christmas Eve. But when I was at Chelsea I could go through the menu, wine and all, 'phone home for hours, entertain friends, all on the club. If I run up a 2p 'phone call with Burnley I get the bill. Keeps your feet on the ground that, I'm telling you.—**Colin Waldron**.

If it was permitted I would love to play in England. Leeds I like, because I like Allan Clarke. I like his way of playing.—**Johann Cruyff**.

I shall continue to give relegated Luton my support—in fact I'm wearing it at this very moment. Some people think it's just the way I walk.—**Eric Morecambe**.

I would look at the First Division table and feel like trying to get in touch with God. Then I'd look at the state of our telephone exchange, and realise there was not much chance there either.—**Harry Haslam**, Luton Town manager.

Husband wanted who understands nothing about football, and who will swear, when married, never to utter a single word about football. Write Box 89, Buenos Aires Presse.

If you think that giving a television interview is just sitting in an armchair dressed up like a dog's dinner, drinking gin and tonic, and saying the first daft thought that comes into your head, then you're about as far off the mark as it's possible to be.—**Malcolm Macdonald**, Newcastle United.

At the ITV Cup final my enjoyment was considerably impaired by an occasional high-pitched whine on my television set. On ringing up to complain I was told it was Alan Ball.—**Scouse Benny**.

Epsom again fell foul of a bad referee who insisted on penalising them for all their fouls.—*Epsom and Ewell Advertiser*.

The TV football analysts' seasonal scuffle with the English language continues: 'scores' continue to be 'scorelines', 'tackles' to be 'scything'. ... The factotum adverb is still 'well' ('Hibbitt did well—didn't he do well—oh, he did do well'). If a player isn't doing well, or does something badly, he is invariably described as unlucky: 'he was very unlucky there' or simply 'oh ... unlucky.'—**Martin Amis**.

When the Amadeus String Quartet play to a sold-out Festival Hall, 5 per cent of all the audience know what it's all about—who have played quartets themselves and can empathise. When West Ham play to a sold-out Upton Park, 75 per cent know what it's all about.—**Hans Keller**.

Players in Greece can earn far more selling games than winning them. Everything has a price. You don't need coaches in Greece, you need cashiers.—**Joe Mallet**, former Greek coach.

The crowd think that Todd handled the ball then ... they must have seen something that nobody else did.—**Barry Davies**.

What Best didn't realise until it was too late was that whereas Paul McCartney could stay up till the small hours and then write a pop song about it, George simply found it more difficult to keep himself at a level of fitness required in a top athlete.—**Michael Parkinson**.

The rules of soccer are very simple. Basically, if it moves, kick it; if it doesn't move, kick it until it does.—**Phil Woosnam**, explaining the game to Americans.

I did the ordinary things that ordinary managers do, like reshaping the youth scheme. But on the whole I am far above the ordinary.—**Malcolm Allison**.

In Match of the Day, Jimmy Hill does his modern version of that favourite medieval theological exercise—debating how many angels could sit on the head of a pin. But with him, it's called 'Did he fall or was he pushed?' It involves slow motion, psychology, and elementary physics, and is conducted with such straight-faced fervour that it is hard to remember that he is talking of the momentary grounding of a gladiator rather than the downfall of empires.—**Shaun Usher**.

The Minister of Football, Mr Dennis Tharg, yesterday outlined his shock charter to combat what he called 'this malignant cancer that is destroying the name of Neasden FC'. Among the measures he proposes are: 1, Solid electric fencing 50 ft high; 2, Individual observation cells to separate both fans; 3, Passports and surety of £1,000 per fan, returnable at the whistle; 4, Major laser-beam brain surgery to diminish aggressive instincts; 5, Inspector Knacker to be provided with special iron-tipped boot, capable of being brought into contact at a moment's notice with sensitive areas of the body; 6, 100-fathom deep moat, patrolled by nuclear-powered submarines and piranha sharks.—**Lord Gnome**.

THORNHILL BAPTISTS 1, BRAISHFIELD 1:
Baptists started with 10 men. Mick Harfield arrived late and made the 11 despite his tragic news that his wife had passed away the same morning. Everyone was stunned and at half-time two minutes' silence was observed. Mick was a hero indeed to stay for the duration of the match.—*Romsey Advertiser*, March 21.

FIT AND WELL: Mrs Rosina Harfield asks us to point out that last week's report of the Braishfield football match was completely untrue. She is fit and well.—*Romsey Advertiser*, March 27.

My mother's success is akin to Germany winning the World Cup.—**Mark Thatcher**.

1976

I was potentially quite bright at school, but when they'd be telling me about the reproduction of the spyrogyra, all I was thinking was how to get a left-back to overlap.—**Malcolm Macdonald**.

Mr Tom Whattle, a Chelsea supporter, was fined £10 on Monday for sticking a hot dog up the anus of a police horse called Eileen. 'I was overcome with excitement after the match. I am a genuine animal lover,' he told the court.—*Fulham Chronicle*.

Mike Smith treats us like men. He doesn't try to organise cinema outings for us. He achieves discipline in a responsible way, without instilling fear into players like Don Revie did at Leeds.—**Terry Yorath**, captain of Wales XI.

The Stoke City defender has knee and thing injuries.
—The *Guardian*.

For those of you with black-and-white sets, Liverpool are in the all-red strip.—**David Coleman**.

If the meek are going to inherit the earth, then the Oxford defence look like being land barons.—Overheard at Iffley Road.

There's a whiff of the bazaar about the FA. An England team manager should not syndicate half-ghosted banalities; less still when they become controversial. England's shirts should not have become sold or changed.—**Brian Glanville**.

Since giving up First Division soccer I feel like a decent human being again. We were remote. You couldn't walk around a shop in town without thinking all eyes were on you. Now when old men come up to me I want to talk about simple things, about trees and flowers. If you like I've found out what it's like to stand and stare again. I'm not particularly religious, but now I want to start going to church again and sing in the choir.—**Alan Hinton**, former Derby County winger.

Professionalism is, if you like, not having sex on Thursdays or Fridays.—**Don Revie**.

Really, I should have brought back Moore and Greaves for the Italy match.—**Don Revie**.

If I were the directors of Admiral I'd be looking for a get-out clause in the clothing contract before the England team did our product any more damage.—**Michael Parkinson**.

Italy's second goal was the ultimate answer to Revie's dossiers—'watch Causio, he is apt to leap two feet in the air as he receives a pass, sell a dummy while doing so, flick the ball past a defender with an instep and disappear with a puff of smoke'.—**David Lacey**.

1977

A Private Eye inquiry has unearthed disturbing facts which raise searing question marks over the head of Neasden soccer supremo, Ron Knee, 59. After years of inner turmoil, Dollis Hill manager Bob Stockhausen has at last spoken out over his moment of shame—'It was just before the match in the gents' toilet at the Cohen Arms, Tesco Road, when the ashen faced mastermind approached me and said "Can I have a word with you"?' Knee then made highly improper suggestions, Stockhausen alleges.—**E. I. Addio**.

Football in the 1970s is very rewarding financially and can provide the opportunity to travel to almost any country in the world.—**Don Revie**, in *The Soccer Diary 1977*.

People have been making money out of me.—**Don Revie**.

Geddes has scored: He kept his head even though he's got a cut over his right eye.—**John Motson**.

Sir Alf Ramsey was once a player's player and is now a gentleman's gentleman.—**A. S. Lias**.

Tottenham's merciless thrashing of Bristol Rovers wasn't really Spurs' victory as far as John Motson was concerned: all he could think of as the goals mounted was whether or not the Match of the Day record was going to be broken: at least a minor coronary seemed on the cards as his strangulated shrieks reached falsetto territories hitherto uncharted. When number nine went in I'm sure I heard something drop.—**Ian Hamilton**.

My advice to my successor is to get a settled team as soon as possible and stick to it.—**Don Revie**.

On our Nottingham Forest team coach the radio dial always points to Radio 4, not Radio 1's pop. Show me a talented player who is thick and I will show you a player who has problems.—**Brian Clough**.

I used to stand up and glare around when fans were giving Geoff stick and they all used to shout: 'Wasn't me, Mrs Hurstie, wasn't me ...' Geoff told me again and again to hold my tongue. Norman Hunter's mum used to lash out with her handbag when people booed her Norm.—**Mrs Geoff Hurst**.

Mr Thomas Haycock, a goalkeeper, has been dropped from the Greentown BME XI after their failure to win a match in four seasons of 'uphill football'. Mr Haston Lash, Greentown's manager, said yesterday: 'Haycock's game fell to pieces after the team began calling him "Cheesecake". I know that he weighs 20 stone and that top-of-the-net work upsets him. Nevertheless, he has let in 107 goals in three matches.' Mr Haycock said: 'Why blame me? If the team worked together I would have nothing to do. Instead they began to call me "cheesecake" when the ball was flashing around me. We were only losing 17–0 at half-time. They gave up too easily.' Before leaving the club house he said he would do his utmost to regain his place.—**Christopher Logue**, *Yorkshire Post*.

Even now a team of linguists is at work translating Don Revie's writings on the game from the original gibberish into Arabic.—**Michael Parkinson**.

Kuwait has placed an order with a British firm to supply 25,000 footballs—but stipulated that they must be delivered inflated. Mercury International of Longton said they would ship out the balls deflated to save cargo space, but would send out a special team to blow up the things after unloading.—Reuter report.

Exchange in Rome court: Italian prosecutor—'You are charged with being drunk and disorderly last night. How do you plead?' Liverpool supporter—'Liverpool Magico!' Case dismissed.

The ideal soccer board of directors should be made up of three men—two dead and the other dying.—**Tommy Docherty**.

To the world at large, the little grey-haired lady looks like everyone's idea of the perfect librarian. But beneath the calm, bookish appearance of Mrs Anne Evans, Aberystwyth librarian, there beats a passionate heart. She has a secret love. For Mrs Evans is such an Arsenal fanatic that she even arranges the books on her shelves so that the covers make a bank of red and white. On match days she too always wears red and white clothes—though she also changes her outfit to yellow and blue when Arsenal have to wear their away strip.—*Sunday People*.

I asked Ron Knee how he saw the future now his side had not qualified. 'We must start again from scratch,' he said, 'throw out the dossiers, and concentrate on essentials like equipping the squad with proper spectacles and deaf aids so they are fully responsive to each others position on and off the ball at any given moment in time.'—**E. I. Addio**.

For a footballer, it's like living in a box. Someone takes you out of the box to train and play ... and makes all your decisions. I have seen players, famous internationals, in an airport lounge all get up and follow one bloke to the lav. Six of them maybe, all standing there not wanting a piss themselves, but following the bloke who does. Like sheep.—**Geoff Hurst**.

The sumptuous and singular footballistic stage which is under construction at Mar del Plata has now reached 75 per cent of its total erection.—**Argentine World Cup Organising Committee**.

There are only two basic situations in football. Either you have the ball or you haven't.—**Ron Greenwood**.

1978

The world of soccer was rocked to its foundations yesterday when an ashen-faced Ron Knee, 59, broke down and told a High Court judge that everything he had said was 'a pack of lies in the strictly legal sense of the phrase'. His tight lips trembling for the first time in living memory, the controversial Neasden supremo told the jury, 'I did not lie deliberately. It just came natural.' Later, following a showdown meeting, club chairman, Brig. Buffy Cohen, said: 'We are standing behind Big Ron 100 per cent. Ron told me at the outset he was an incompetent drunken liar and every word he said is true.'—**E. I. Addio**, Our Man in the Visitors' Gallery with the Yorkie Bar and the *Sporting Life*.

I feel ashamed for myself and Scotland, but I do not think that some of the Scottish team have the brains to feel ashamed.—**Martin Buchan**.

After enjoying Ipswich winning the Cup Final Mrs Thatcher was asked on Radio 2 who was her Man of the Match. Without hesitation she replied 'The Number Ten shirt, Trevor Whymark'. Her erring staff had neglected to point out to her that though Whymark was listed in the programme, he was in fact injured and did not play.—*Daily Mail.*

If, as every Englishman suspects, the Scots ingest a weakness for hyperbole with their mother's milk, Ally MacLeod would seen to have been breast-fed until he was 15.—**Hugh McIlvanney.**

Nothing can be wholly bad, even football … a girl told me that football on the telly was driving her up the wall. In anguish she tried BBC-2 to be greeted by a film in Swedish with letters along the bottom. Finally she had to resort to a desperate remedy to fill the aching vacuum. She went to bed with a book. So the World Cup may yet trigger off an astonishing revival in the art of the novel.—**John Mortimer.**

Sir,—You state that Brooke Bond Oxo is using Mrs Ally MacLeod in advertisements for tea. This is not so. We use chimps to promote our world cup. Yours etc, D. F. Barnett, Deputy Managing Director.—Letter in the *Guardian.*

At the end of **La ci darem la mano,** the famous Don Giovanni duettino, the music, now in a rather speedy Siciliano rhythm, virtually turns into its opposite: unity is achieved by a complementary contrast. Let that master be my model for a concluding tribute to another master of wordless logic—West Ham's Trevor Brooking at Upton Park on Saturday.—**Hans Keller,** *Spectator.*

In reply to your question, What is always brought to Cup finals but never used? (the loser's ribbons that are tied to the cup), the answer should surely be 'Malcolm Macdonald'.—**Laurence Lebor**.

The world of soccer was rocked to its foundations last night by the news that Neasden soccer supremo Ron Knee, 59, had clinched a multi-million pound deal to buy Argentine-born Hernan dez de les Pretwinkle, 46. Ashen-faced Knee told the press: 'How did I do it? Simple. I tracked him down to a hairdressing salon in Tesco Road and made him an offer he could not refuse, to wit a life's supply of Boston's Rio de Janeiro Junta-style Knockout Stout.'—**E. I. Addio**, Our Man in the Books and Mags Shop with the Dark Glasses.

A nun, Collette Duveen, of the Order of the Merciful Sisters, was arrested for kicking in the teeth a lorry driver who cheered when Holland scored their second goal in the World Cup final.—*News of the World*.

I only took two tablets.—**Willie Johnston**.

Our problem is that we've tried to score too many goals.—**Gordon Lee**, Everton Manager.

HANDY PHRASES: Dejen de torturarme, por favor (Please stop torturing me). Mi periodico les pagara bien si me dejen ir (My newspaper will pay well if you let me go). Per favor entregen mi cuerpo a mi familia (Please deliver my body to my family).—NUJ handbook to journalists covering World Cup.

I think it is a happy coincidence that the ball is the instrument of the sport represented by FIFA. It is round without angles or sharp edges. With its unlimited surface, lines may criss-cross to infinity. When in motion it can be impelled in all directions with no deformation and without losing its characteristics. To fulfill its performance it is necessary never to be still, always on the move. I feel you can take it as a symbol of my work as your president of FIFA.—**Joao Havelange**.

Four minutes to half-time; one–one; whoever scores now will go in with an advantage.—**Hugh Johns**, ITV.

There's been a colour clash; both teams arrived wearing white.—**John Motson**.

If those West Ham defenders weren't sleeping, they were certainly slumbering.—**John Motson**.

Standing still is the same as going backwards, and when you do that people are bound to overtake you.—**Ian Wolstenholme**, Harlow FC manager.

I am convinced that Laurie Cunningham is the greatest talent we have ever seen in this country, and I include Stan Matthews and George Best.—**George Petchey**, Millwall manager.

1979

I would willingly sacrifice five hours of Keegan for five minutes of Best at his peak.—**David Lacey**.

Ten years is a long time ... in the first months of 1970 I was behind the simmering goal net in Mexico. It was all over before it had begun, like a short Disney cartoon. Jairzinho's rushing centre, Pele heading fiercely down towards the gaping hole left by Banks, guarding the near post. Then Banks in an attitude of a praying mantis spinning on to a new twig, played the ball up and away with an extended palm into oblivion. The ball tumbled over the goal and rolled slowly down on the other side with the sudden abatement of an ocean wave after breaking on a rock. ... In the last fortnight of 1979 Gordon Banks was sacked as Port Vale's reserve team coach.—**John Moynihan**.

Talks over Dave Watson's transfer are being hampered by the Bremen officials' lack of decent English.—**Peter Swales**, Manchester City chairman.

When I know you better, Thompson, I'll call you Sir Harold.—**Don Revie**.

It will take five years for the American League to come up with a great US soccer player. That's how long it takes for naturalisation, isn't it?—**Rinus Michels,** coach to Los Angeles Aztecs.

In 1966 when England won the World Cup we were all watching the final on television at Binkie Beaumont's in mounting excitement. The suspense was very great. At the end we all stood up and cheered, and tears were seen to be running down Sir John Gielgud's cheeks. He brushed them away and then said something very characteristic of him: 'Sorry to make such an ass of myself, but I find it very moving when anything at all goes right for once for dear little England.'—**Arthur Marshall.**

I've never made a cup of tea for a man. If George wants a cup of tea he knows he has to make it himself.—**Mrs Angela Best.**

When he first came to Forest, Trevor Francis thought he had a stamina problem. He was full of rubbish about wanting to wear a certain number on his shirt. We've got rid of that nonsense and made a man of him. Also, he now heads the ball occasionally.—**Peter Taylor.**

Coventry City can beat anybody on the day, but also they can lose against anybody on the day.—**Emlyn Hughes**, BBC.

Mr Bob Coke, captain of Kirkham Carpet Works FC, explained: 'It defiled the annals of sport. We were beating Bissmore Rovers by 19–0 after two of their players had walked off the pitch, saying they were going to Amsterdam, and Wally Moore, their centre-half, was asleep behind the goal. Suddenly, Mr Sid Hopkins, their trainer, drove his transit van across the pitch. The Rovers all jumped aboard. They picked up Moore and vanished into the blue. Next day I had a note with a signature I could not read, saying that Bissmore had disbanded and wishing Kirkham bad luck.—**Christopher Logue**, *Express & Star*.

Postman David Coleman, who streaked naked from the waist down before a 30,000 crowd during the Wolves–Coventry game on November 17, was fined today £25. He told the court: 'It was a very boring match.'—*Evening News*.

Nottingham Forest players average £22,000 a year, an hourly rate of £35 for playing and training. Top players in Germany and Italy average twice that, while in Spain the hourly rate is a mouth-watering £97.—**John Parsons**.

My players may be suffering from pre-season tiredness.—**Malcolm Allison**.

This case has been as much of an ordeal as losing three Cup finals in one day. I stand in that witness box and look out at Elsie and the two kids, see what they're suffering, and it just drains you. But I had to go through with it.—**Don Revie**.

1980

If anyone wants my job they've got to take it away from me over my dead body.—**Ernie Walley**, Saturday, November 29.

If I can work with anyone I can certainly work with Malcolm.—**Ernie Walley**, Sunday, November 30.

All the team are 100 per cent behind the manager, but I can't speak for the rest of the squad.—**Brian Greenhoff**, Radio Leeds.

Because, rather surprisingly, our local newspaper did not report it, we are printing my speech of welcome to His Royal Highness, the Duke of Edinburgh, for all those supporters who could not be present when he officially opened the Sky Blue Sports Centre.—**Jimmy Hill** in Coventry City programme.

PC Swithun, who made a record number of 49 arrests at Second Division Shrewsbury last season, has been snapped up by the London Met and will turn out for them at the next Arsenal match. 'It's sad leaving Salop, but I feel ready for the big time,' he said yesterday.—*Punch*.

He was the real thorn in Thistle's flesh.—**David Francey**, Radio Scotland.

Liverpool always seem to find a boot at the right moment to keep Birmingham City at arm's length.—**Clive Tilsley**, Radio City.

1981
A manager must buy cheap and sell dear. Another manager rings me to ask about a player. 'He's great,' I say, 'super lad, goes to church twice a day, good in the air, two lovely feet, make a great son-in-law.' You never tell them he couldn't trap a bag of cement.—**Tommy Docherty**.

And now, the familiar sight of Liverpool raising the League Cup for the first time.—**Brian Moore**.

Yurggggh! Der stod Ingelland. Lord Nelson! Lord Beaverbrook! Winston Churchill! Henry Cooper! Clement Attlee! Anthony Eden! Lady Diana! Der stod dem all! Der stod dem all! Maggie Thatcher, can you hear me? Can you hear me Maggie? Your boys take one hell of a beating tonight.—**Borg Lillelien**, Norwegian World Cup commentator.

With the very last kick of the game Macdonald scored with a header.—**Allan Parry**.

Graham Rix was not so much off colour yesterday as not quite on song.—**Jimmy Hill**.

Grand Double Horror Bill Tonight: Jaws 2, and England v. Switzerland soccer.—Notice outside Glasgow video theatre.

1982
Mariner and Butcher there, trying to work the oracle on the near post.—**Martin Tyler**.

Being given chances and not taking them, that's what life is all about.—**Ron Greenwood**.

The announcement of the disqualification was greeted by booze from the spectators at the pool.—*Gloucestershire Echo*.

The soccer world was rocked to its foundations today when Ron Knee, 59, the ashen-faced supremo of Neasden FC announced his new all-black squad to meet Dollis Hill. Of his clear-out of his former squad, Knee said, 'With all due respect to the giants of the past, you cannot play well in wheelchairs, let alone from open prison where some are awaiting trial for mass rape. We have to look to the future.'—**E. I. Addio**.

And Wilkins sends an inch-perfect pass to no one in particular.—**Bryon Butler**.

1983
There is a rat in the camp trying to throw a spanner in the works.—**Chris Cattlin**, Brighton manager.

Canon League? Some teams are so negative they could be sponsored by Kodak.—**Tommy Docherty**.

A professional footballer has a duty to his wife and family to earn as much as he can from this sport as quickly as he can.—**John Wark** of Ipswich on why his £50,000 salary is not enough.

They have brought this town into disrepute, making Wolverhampton the butt of every comedian's joke. We must have talks as soon as possible to find out where Allied Properties' interests really lie. On Saturday's performance it is not in football.—**John Bird**, Wolverhampton Council leader, after Wolves' 5–0 defeat by Watford.

Only women and horses work for nothing.—**Doug Ellis**, Aston Villa's first paid director.

No one has a divine right to being employed by this club.—**Peter Hill-Wood**, Arsenal chairman, three weeks before sacking Terry Neill.

I sat in my car one day, first in line when the lights changed. I stopped and instinctively everyone behind stopped in sequence. I realised that football was that simple. My team played a marvellous eight-man move last week and one of the kids turned and shouted, 'Traffic lights'. I could have kissed him.—**Alan Ball**, Portsmouth youth coach.

It may have been an awful night, but the meat and potato pies were brill.—**Away Traveller** in the Crewe Alexandra Supporters' Association newsletter, on a visit to Halifax.

We hope to revive the old tradition of the husband going to football on Christmas Day while the wives cook the turkey.—**Eric White**, Brentford official.

We pass each other on the A52 going to work most days of the week. But if his car broke down and I saw him thumbing a lift, I wouldn't pick him up—I'd run him over.—**Brian Clough** on Peter Taylor.

I know it's a bad time to walk out on a job in football. But I have been putting so little into the job and taking so much out that if I hadn't resigned I would have been taking money under false pretences.—**John Bond** on leaving Manchester City.

My wife has been magic about it.—**Bond** when the story of his affair with a City employee broke two days after he resigned.

John Bond has blackened my name with his insinuations about the private lives of all football managers. Both my wives are upset.—**Malcolm Allison**.

This surface is the best thing that ever happened to English football.—**Malcolm Allison** after Middlesbrough's 6–1 defeat on QPR's Omniturf.

If we go all the way to Wembley, it's difficult to imagine the club looking elsewhere for a new manager.—**Mike Bamber**, Brighton chairman, on Jimmy Melia's employment prospects in March 1983.

We might have got to Wembley, but you've got to remember we've only won seven out of 36 League games under Jimmy.—**Brighton director** on why Melia was dismissed in October.

The politics involved make me nostalgic for the Middle East.—**Henry Kissinger** after FIFA rejected US bid to stage World Cup.

It wasn't so much the death threats or the vandalism, but when you sit with your family in the directors' box and hear a couple of thousand people chanting 'Gilbert Blades is a wanker', then you feel it's time to go.—**Gilbert Blades**, after resigning Lincoln chairmanship.

All the lads have been moaning about him. He dives in yards from the ball and hits you on the legs whether the ball's there or not. No one appreciates that kind of thing, especially in training.—**Anonymous Brighton footballer** on Hans Craay Jr, suspended in Holland but on trial at Brighton.

I've heard claims that I'm supposed to be using Mafia money. Some football clubs are in such a mess right now you could buy them out of Brownie funds.—**Anton Johnson**, then Rotherham chairman, on his part in club takeovers.

I find it ironical that Brian Clough should call for a total ban (on TV soccer) after making the kind of money as a member of TV's World Cup panel that would seem a pools win to small clubs.—**Derek Dougan**.

My only problem seems to be with the Italian breakfasts. No matter how much money you've got you can't seem to get any Rice Krispies.—**Luther Blissett** just after his transfer to Milan.

I'll put my money where my mouth is and bet anyone we stay in the First Division.—**Graham Hawkins**, Wolves manager, in August.

Blimey, the ground looks a bit different to Watford.
Where's the dog track?—**Blissett** at San Siro Stadium.

When the League offered us 31 matches live, we said: 'Can
you deliver?' The answer was: 'Anything can be delivered,
so long as the money's right.' I was shattered that they
could believe that money is more important than the
welfare of the game.—**Cliff Morgan**, BBC Head of Outside
Broadcasts.

I'm sure the top clubs would be magnanimous and give
some of the money to the small clubs, but it's essential that
we keep the lion's share.—**Douglas Alexiou**, Spurs'
chairman, on the threat of breakaway negotiations by the
big clubs.

Looking back, some of the pictures I've posed for have
been daft.—**Charlie Nicholas.**

Agents do nothing for the good of football. I'd like to see
them lined up against a wall and machine-gunned . . . some
accountants and solicitors along with them.—**Graham
Taylor**, Watford manager.

We looked bright all week in training, but the problem
with football is that Saturday always comes along.—**Keith
Burkinshaw**, Spurs manager.

I apologised afterwards to Roberts. He's a hard man
himself and understands these things. I'm sure he'll get his
own back over the next five years.—**Andy Gray**, after
injuring Spurs' Graham Roberts.

In terms of a 15-round boxing match, we're not getting past the first round. The tempo is quicker. Teams will pinch your dinner from under your noses. They don't give you a chance to play. If you don't heed the warnings, you get nailed to the cross.—**Gordon Milne**, Leicester manager, on the First Division.

It's getting to the stage when we hate them and they dislike us.—**Kenny Sansom** on referees.

I was wrong to sign for Mr Clough. I'd heard of his reputation—but I just don't understand him. We rarely see the manager during the week, but we can find him in the papers every day.—**Frans Thijssen**.

They came for warfare, to cause trouble and fight. It's been said that they're a small minority. They are not. There were 1,700 of them and nearly all of them were at it.—**Bert Millichip**, FA chairman, on England fans in Luxembourg.

When Robson's name was mentioned as a candidate for the England job, I dismissed it as a joke. Now that joke's become a reality, and it isn't funny.—**Malcolm Allison**.

I admire English football. Your players have everything that is necessary to be successful. But you don't always use all the possibilities. Maybe an outsider could introduce a more effective system.—**Sepp Piontek**, Denmark manager.

Tottenham's supporters were exemplary, the sort of guests we always like to have here.—**Bayern Munich official**.

With about two minutes to go I looked across at their bench, and I thought, 'When the whistle goes, I'm going to go across there, shake hands and say, "All the best", and then when they've gone in I'm going to go mad'.—**Alan Buckley**, Walsall manager after winning at Arsenal.

1984

An announcement will shortly be made after the interim measures to be taken to undertake certain of his duties pending discussions after any future staff appointment.—**Barnsley FC spokesman** on vacant manager's job after sacking of Norman Hunter.

There was a lad standing in front of me when it happened and, you know, these old eyes of mine. . . .—**Joe Fagan**, Liverpool manager, after the refusal of an Everton penalty appeal.

The Giro Cup Final.—Merseyside fan's description of the Everton v. Liverpool Milk Cup final at Wembley, in Granada TV's Home & Away.

I'm in the electric chair now.—**Bobby Collins** on succeeding Hunter.

My apologies to you all for supporting us through a trying season.—**Vince Barker**, Hartlepool United chairman, in his final programme notes for 1983–84.

Even his feet are intelligent.—**Michel Hidalgo**, French manager, on Platini.

In the battle of zone defences, both sides showed their holes. But when Liverpool closed theirs, they did so with greater authority, often knocking opponents to the turf.—**Associated Press agency report** on Roma v. Liverpool.

Tottenham will get a new manager and after he's had three or four wins, Keith Burkinshaw will be forgotten.—**Burkinshaw,** after leading Spurs to the UEFA Cup in his final game.

I analyse the whole situation. I have the chance most often of choosing the right solution and having the skill to apply it. I have a very good right foot and a good little left foot, and I'm not bad with my head either. I can defend too, if needs.—**Michel Platini,** captain of France's European Championship winning team.

As far as he is concerned, he is God. There is nobody around big enough to tell *him* what to do.—**Margaret Atkinson,** wife of Man United manager Ron, after news broke of his extra-marital affair.

Half an hour? You could shoot Ben Hur in half an hour. You've got 15 seconds.—**Ron Atkinson** to photographer who asked for 30 minutes with Manchester United manager.

Balloon ball. The percentage game. Route One ... It's crept into the First Division. We get asked to lend youngsters to these teams. We won't do it. They come back with bad habits: big legs and good eyesight.—**Ron Atkinson** on soccer's long-ball game.

It's like the difference between a soldier walking through Aldershot and one walking through Belfast. There's a state of mind necessary for the latter if you're to survive.—**Howard Wilkinson**, Sheffield Wednesday manager, on the difference between First and Second Divisions.

Managers in the Third and Fourth Divisions have chips on their shoulders because they think they should be in better jobs. They go about whingeing all day.—**Jimmy Greaves**.

I thought he'd gone back on the drink.—**John McGovern**, Bolton manager, replying to Greaves.

On a boys' night out after a game the most I'll have is seven or eight pints of lager. That to me isn't being drunk.—**Charlie Nicholas**.

He gets lots of women after him and when sex is offered on a plate he takes it. He wants to play the field.—**Suzanne Dando**, ex-Olympic gymnast and girlfriend of Charlie Nicholas.

Tommy Docherty criticising Charlie Nicholas is like Bernard Manning telling Jimmy Tarbuck to clean up his act.—**Gordon Taylor**, players' union secretary.

We went to Porto and there's a bloody hurricane. We come here and the shops are shut. That's our fate. When we play in Russia, Reagan will probably have blown the place up.—**Jim Steel**, Wrexham centre forward.

Heno, mae tref wylaidd Wrecsam yn croesawu Rhufain odidog ... Daeth y Rhufeiniwr hanesyddol hwnnw, Julius Caesar, adref o'i ymweliad cyntaf a Phrydain a'r geiriau enwog 'Veni, Vidi, Vici'. Gobeithio na chaiff hanes ei ailadrodd!—**W. P. Griffiths**, Wrexham chairman, in programme, welcome to Roma.

Chelsea have watched Gordon Davies more times than they've watched Coronation Street.—**Ernie Clay**, Fulham chairman.

Charlie Nicholas? Seems like he's getting a lot of everything except the ball.—**Jimmy Greaves** on Nicholas's poor display during the televised Sheffield Wednesday v. Arsenal match.

When I arrived in Bahrain they all looked the same off the field. Now I've sorted out the Abdullahs from the Mustaphas.—**Keith Burkinshaw**.

When I arrived in the summer, one of my predecessors told the Spanish press that Meester Terry would be gone by Christmas. He forgot to say which year.—**Terry Venables**.

There was an element of the old Leeds United professionalism out there. Terry Gibson was whacked in the face ... then he retaliated against a player who pulled his hair.—**Bobby Gould**, Coventry manager, complaining about the West Brom side run by Giles, Hunter and Stiles.

I'm very flattered.—**Johnny Giles**.

Hello Don, no deal.—**Jim Gregory**, QPR chairman, in four-word phone call to Don Revie about manager's job.

I thought it was 19–0. I must have lost count.—**Alex Smith**, Stirling Albion manager, after a 20–0 win over Selkirk.

They should make Leeds play all their away matches at home.—**Billy Hamilton**, Oxford striker, after rioting by Leeds United fans.

The main thing I miss about London? The sausages. Not much else.—**Terry Venables**, Barcelona and ex-QPR manager.

I told them 'I'm glad I didn't have you four defending me when I had my court case. The judge would've put his black cap on.'—**Tommy Docherty** on his Wolves defence.

The lad's got concussion and loss of memory. He doesn't remember giving away their second goal.—**John Neal**, Chelsea manager, on defender Joe McLaughlin after a defeat at Newcastle.

1985

It seems astonishing that 20,000 Scotland fans can stay a week in Spain without one incident, yet we cannot play an international in Britain.—Scottish FA secretary **Ernie Walker** after government pressure to switch the game against England from Wembley to Hampden Park.

Any spectator sport only survives through the bond between those who perform and those who watch. Once a section of the crowd attempts to interfere physically with the action, that trust is broken irrevocably.—**David Lacey**.

His day will come another night.—England manager **Bobby Robson** on Ray Wilkins' performance in a 2–1 defeat of the Republic of Ireland.

Football has put itself into the red through its own fault, the clubs in the main being guided by those having little or no feeling for the game.—**Geoffrey Green**.

International soccer is three steps up the ladder from ordinary League football. Unless you are really fresh you'll struggle . . . it's more demanding, more physical and more pacey.—Manager **Bobby Robson** after England's 0–0 World Cup draw in Romania.

Mark Wright has learned a lot. That he's going to get bumped and bored, that international football is not always about elegance and beautiful play.—**Bobby Robson**.

1971

When I retired I was 22. A swimmer does not get punched or clobbered, no cuts, bruises or broken bones, and I was an amateur not a professional; but I had had it. I was tired and I had been tired for three years.—**Don Schollander**, US champion swimmer.

1972

And there's Brinkley at the back—quite content to let Spitz set the pace.—**BBC swimming commentator**.

Mark Spitz talks a lot about himself. But how can you blame him? That's the only thing people ask him about.—US swimmer, **Dave Edgar**.

1973

The money I've made has no correlation with the validity of my statements.—**Mark Spitz**, millionaire.

1975

Britain's swim girls are just not tough enough. At the world championships they were no more than a glee club for the men.—**Jack Queen**, their coach.

I've taught a young Vietnamese to swim easily, and half-castes too. Even Pakistanis do reasonably well. But Africans just sink. There is no question about it.—**Chris Maloney**, Gloucester swimming coach.

I was delirious, shocked out of my mind at the end. And to think that I had broken the world record too. They raised the Union Jack and played God Save The Queen, and I suddenly realised all the Aussies and Canadians were singing too. I had been thrilled. Now I was touched emotionally. Empire unity, a moment I'll never forget.—**David Wilkie**.

1977

There are two separate women's swimming championships, one for East Germans, one for the rest. You only have to listen to their voices to know why. One of the girls in my squad complained that there were men in the women's changing room at a recent international gala in Vienna, only for the chaperone to discover on investigation that she had merely overheard East German girls in the next cubicle.—**Charles Wilson**, British swimming coach.

1979

It only hurt once—from beginning to end.—**Doc Counsilman**, oldest man to swim the Channel.

1980

This boy swims like a greyhound.—**Athole Still**, ITV.

1982
It's obvious these Russian swimmers are determined to do well on American soil.—**Anita Lonsborough**.

1971

When I got to the final, I asked someone to pinch me to make sure it was really happening.—**Evonne Goolagong** at Wimbledon.

If the ILTF and the WCT were the Russians and Americans we'd all be dead by now.—**John Newcombe**.

For the Davis Cup you have to have separate bedrooms from your husband while he is in training. You spend the whole of the year living with him then all of a sudden they say, 'No, no, naughty, not the night before the Davis Cup'. I suppose it's because they are representing England. —**Mrs Mark Cox**.

1972

I have been banned from umpiring at Wimbledon for not wearing a tie. I've not, in fact, been wearing one there for eight years. I doubt if I'll be back.—Tennis umpire **Gerald Garside**.

I am glad I have not got a big serve—because I fear for the size of my shoulders.—**Françoise Durr**.

Glamorous, huh? Singers can wear gowns to hide the bulges, and wigs and make-up. But our bodies are seen the way they really are. We come off the court sweating, hair dripping. Our life is showering and changing. I change clothes five times a day and wash my hair every day. It's a tough role to play, so you don't see many femmes fatales in tennis dresses.—**Billie Jean King**, on the glamorous life in big-time sports.

If someone says I'm not feminine, I say 'screw it'.—**Rosie Casals**.

Mark Cox is suddenly like the rugby player who has learned to tackle low. He's not afraid to skin his knees these days.—**John Newcombe**.

Billie Jean King's father put her into tennis to stop her being a woman wrestler.—**Jim Murray**, *Angeles Times*.

People go to Laver to talk about tennis—they come to me to talk about abortions.—**Billie Jean King**.

If you put monkeys on to play they'd still pack the Centre Court at Wimbledon.—**Neale Fraser**.

There is someone, somewhere who could do for Virginia Wade what Franz Stampfl did for Roger Bannister.—**Chris Brasher**.

No, I have never been to a psychiatrist. I hate being analysed by friends because they never put you back together again.—**Virginia Wade**.

Margaret Court plays in such run-of-the-mill garments. I reproach her for it and decry her influence on the game and attitude to the public. The stars who don't care a damn how they look are amateurs.—**Teddy Tinling**.

1973

I want to prove that women are lousy. They stink. They don't belong on the same court as a man.—**Bobby Riggs**.

I asked the All England Club for two tickets for friends to watch me in the quarter-finals. I did not mind being refused as much as the manner. It was dreadful—as if I were asking for £100,000. If it had happened a week before I would have walked out with all the others.—**Jan Kodes**.

I owe it all to my wife. She does not like me to be angry on court. So when the ball goes three yards out and the line-judge is asleep, I no longer tell him what I think. I say to myself 'Be calm', and now I am the big sport, yes?—**Ilie Nastase**.

The threat to Wimbledon and Europe is what is going to happen in the States, not poor Nikki Pilic.—**Donald Dell**.

I know what I have to do to survive. I don't go out there to love my enemy. I go out there to squash him.—**Jimmy Connors**.

1974
Inside me, I just go crazy. I mess up a backhand and tell myself, 'You creep', and maybe throw my racket to vent my emotions. Then I see one coming and visualise just where I'm going to hit it, and the shot's perfect—and I feel beautiful all over.—**Billie Jean King**.

All I wish is that Rosewall would get old.—**John Newcombe**.

ATP, WTT, WCT, ILTF—there's everything but the B and O Railroad. It's now as absurd as an Abbott and Costello comedy routine—and look what happened to vaudeville.—**Fred Perry**.

Most of the ILTF are idiots—a bunch of antiquated, unresponsive, self-perpetuating septuagenarians.—**Arthur Ashe**.

Nobody likes me. And I couldn't care a goddam stuff.—**Jimmy Connors**.

He's an animal as a competitor with a good nose for blood ... more savage than anyone since Gonzalez. The vulgarness—the cursing, the fingers, the stroking of the racket like he was masturbating—that's all part of it.—Tennis player **Gene Scott**, about Jimmy Connors.

If you're paid before you walk on the court, what's the point in playing as if your life depended on it? Hell, if you've locked up a bundle of money from a challenge match, you might as well take a vacation the rest of the year.—Former tennis pro **Arthur Ashe**, in opposing the so-called 'Heavyweight Championships of Tennis', when it was disclosed that athletes were to receive prearranged payments regardless of who won or lost.

1975

Mister Bastard to you.—**Jimmy Connors'** reply to swearing spectator.

I *AM* trying, for Chrissake.—**Jimmy Connors**.

The ATP stands for bans, boycotts, and baloney. They are suing me for calling Kramer a piranha. But that's only a small fish. Get that down kid, that's an original. I'm going to expose them for the charlatans they are.—**Bill Riordan**.

I am not sure that I am a good enough Davis Cup player to even be chosen for Britain. If I get into a tight position playing for my country, I can never be sure my nerve will stand the pressure.—**Mark Cox**.

So people keep asking what it is like to win Wimbledon. Well, right after the match, when I walked off the court, they handed me a phone. Lew Hoad, who won Wimbledon twice, was on the other end. He had called from Spain midway through the final, and when he found out I was winning, he just stayed on and kept the line open till it was over. *That* is what it is like to win Wimbledon.—**Arthur Ashe**.

Nastase is a Hamlet who wants to play a clown. He is no good at it. His gags are bad, his timing's terrible, and he never knows how he's going over—which last drawback is the kiss of death to any comic.—**Clive James**.

1976

Why did I lose? No reason, though you might like to know that I got tired, my ears started popping, the rubber came off my shoes, I got cramp, and I lost one of my contact lenses. Other than that I was in great shape.—**Bob Lutz**, after losing at Wimbledon.

Doubles makes me worried: Nastase calls me an SOB every time I miss a shot, whereas Arthur Ashe just says, 'Bad luck, James'. I just can't adjust to a partner.—**Jimmy Connors**.

Playing tennis makes me miss my child's birthday. But as long as the cheques keep coming in I can justify it to myself.—**Mark Cox**.

1977

Grass is out on its own. It's a way of life. I do all my own watering by hand because I like to see where it is going.—**Bob Twynam**, Wimbledon groundsman.

I guess I'm not the same. I don't like to say it, it's weird, but I feel sort of different since I got my picture in the newspapers. ... Like I'll be driving my car and some guy will cut me off, you know, and I'll think to myself, just who is this guy, cutting me off? When did he ever get his picture in the paper? It's like I know I'm not just a nobody anymore.—**John McEnroe**.

The proper method of playing mixed doubles is to hit the ball accidentally at the woman opponent as hard and as accurately as possible. Male players must not only retain equanimity on their side of the net, but create dissension on the other.—**Art Hoppe**, US writer/coach.

Nastase's new contract is 35 pages long and 15 of them are devoted to penalties about his behaviour.—**Jerry Buss**, manager of the Los Angeles Strings.

At the end I couldn't hear what the Queen was saying to me. But it was just great to see her lips moving.—**Virginia Wade**.

I hate to lose more than I like to win. I hate to see the happiness on their faces when they beat me.—**Jimmy Connors**, runner-up to Bjorn Borg in the 1977 Pepsi Grand Slam tennis tournament, a result repeated at Wimbledon that same year.

I wonder if she knows what's going on yet. That's great. She's winning. Wait'll she learns how to choke.—**Billie Jean King** on the 14-year-old Tracy Austin.

I don't seem to use my intelligence intelligently.
—**Virginia Wade**.

I think I feel emotion more than most players. I have a drive, a burning desire to win every time I step on court ... I don't have the serve of Martina [Navratilova] or the speed of Rosie [Casals], so I compensate.—**Chris Evert**, before she was eliminated in a lacklustre performance at Wimbledon.

1978
Whoever stole it is spending less money than my wife.—**Ilie Nastase** on his failure to report the theft of his American Express card.

During the course of Wimbledon Dan Maskell said 'Ooh I say' a total of 1,358 times. The trouble with Dan's style is that it's so infectious. Ooh I say, it's a really infectious style.—**Clive James**.

Not since Betty Grable has so much been written about a pair of legs as John Lloyd's. Nastase's agent told me, in a fit of jealousy, that he hopes Lloyd gets varicose veins.—**Taki**.

Umpires at Wimbledon seem to take pleasure in ignoring the pathetic, gesticulating Nastase when he asks them to explain their rather dubious decisions. Why is it part of an umpire's duties to treat a fellow being with such contempt? I suppose that umpires, whose duties seem to consist principally of saying 'Thirtay, fortay' and things like that, have to cultivate feelings of self-importance to make their business seem worthwhile.—**Alexander Chancellor**.

I'll chase that son of a bitch Borg to the ends of the earth. I'll be waiting for him. I'll dog him everywhere. Every time he looks round he'll see my shadow.—**Jimmy Connors**.

I'm kind of bitter about people saying I did this to make money. It just isn't so. I was pretty well off as a physician, and I'm pretty poor as a tennis pro.—Transsexual **Renee Richards**. Richards went back to ophthalmology in 1981.

If Borg nips about the centre court with Brillo Pads under his arms who cares? But if at Virginia's dynamic serve the cameras zoom in on a hairy female armpit Wimbledon would never be the same again.—**Val Hennessey**, *Evening News*.

1979

Sir,—After 50 years' playing tennis I know that when your opponent makes a line call and includes your name, watch out! Whenever you hear him say 'Just out, Bill!' or 'Sorry, Alice, a little long!' get ready for the rip-off. He is in doubt about the call, but knows that when you hear your name mentioned you'll automatically think 'Anyone who is that friendly and personal wouldn't shaft me'. Friend, you've been had!—Letter in *World Tennis*.

In the fourth and fifth sets I won all the big points, every single one. I don't know how, but at Wimbledon I am always winning these points. It's very strange.—**Bjorn Borg**.

Richard loves Ellen very much for the right reasons. They will marry, live happily ever after and he will beat her at tennis.—Advertisement in personal column of *NY Times*.

My greatest strength is that I have no weaknesses.—**John McEnroe**.

About Wimbledon I understand next to nothing and enjoy everything. The great herbaceous border of faces, the wet greens and worn greens and lime juice cordial greens. The services which make the white lines smoke and the wicked low camera angle which stretches out the court like chewing gum. The flood of late sun, the little breeze, and men playing doubles with their own long-legged shadows. And the pain of anguish that rings across the screen when the BBC stop dead at eight right in the middle of, say, the Lloyd brothers doubles. God may forgive them but I would advise them against it.—**Nancy Banks-Smith**.

McEnroe claims John Lloyd is more popular than him because Lloyd married Chris Evert. McEnroe wouldn't be popular if he was married to Marie Osmond.—**Terry Kelleher**, US TV.

In the 1960s, when Billie Jean, Court, Casals and Susman took over, they were bursting with belligerence, full of inferiority complexes, ferocious as boys. They fought my girls like wildcats ... not about the frocks, but about the attitudes they represented.—**Teddy Tinling**.

Imagine the ultimate in hypothetical tennis matches, Gonzales and Hoad v. Connors and McEnroe. Connors, his beady eyes intercepting the bridge of his nose, his tasselled socks swinging in the wind, his prince-valiant haircut ditto, his Freudian swagger. And McEnroe playing tough guy. Gonzo, the closest thing to a death machine come alive, and Hoadie, a study in controlled fury, would fix them with their hatchet looks and there would be nothing their business managers or mothers would be able to do to help them except change their underwear after the match.—**Taki**.

1980

I prefer golf to tennis; all tennis courts look alike.—**Brad Dillman**.

Everyone says that he [Bjorn Borg] can't volley because his ground strokes are so good. He has learned how to volley. It is not textbook, but who cares. It is such hard work playing against him. So many balls come back. It's like taking too many body punches. You are tired by the end.—**Brian Gottfried**, after losing to Bjorn Borg at Wimbledon, which Borg went on to win.

Simply, my strengths aren't half as good as her weaknesses.—**Debbie Jeavons**, on losing 6–0, 6–0, to Chris Evert.

Borg's won Wimbledon four straight times, and out there he's just lost an 18–16 tie-breaker. You'd think maybe just once he'd let up and just say 'forget it'. But oh, no, no way.—**John McEnroe**.

Tracy just couldn't figure Evonne's game. You see, Tracy couldn't realise that Evonne flows; she doesn't run like the rest of us, she just flows.—**Bob Landsdorp**, Miss Austin's coach.

Now is the time for both players to relax, take their minds off the game and just think about their tactics for the next set.—**Ann Jones**, BBC.

We don't always get from slow motion the pace at which they play.—**John Barrett**, BBC.

1981
McEnroe was especially irascible, and shouted assorted unprintables thirteen different times before earning another on-court audience with the referee. Lady Diana Spencer left the Royal Box during the match. 'The wedding's off,' someone said. 'Her ears are no longer virgin.'—*Sports Illustrated*.

To me life in big-time tennis means carrying large amounts of small change in different currencies to work laundromats wherever I happen to be. I spend more time at nights watching my smalls go round than I do watching television.—**Sue Barker**.

If it's Friday it must be francs

1982
If you're up against a girl with big boobs, bring her to the net and make her hit backhand volleys. It's the hardest shot for the well endowed; like when I used to beat Ann Jones, she could hit under them or over them but never through them.—**Billie Jean King**.

Ah, Wimbledon! Strawberries, cream and champers flowing like hot cakes.—**Radio 2 announcer**.

At Wimbledon there's an A locker room, where all of the top-seeded players dress, and a B locker room, which the qualifiers and the junior players are assigned to. Most of the guys in the B locker room are living on a shoestring, eating cheap food and sharing a tiny flat in Earl's Court with four or five other players. But that gives them a tremendous feeling of camaraderie—it's us against them. I've seen a player come back after beating someone from the A locker room, and everyone will stand up and cheer him.—Veteran qualifier **Erik van Dillen**.

I have given it much thought, and I'm not coming to
Wimbledon this year: I want to watch the World
Cup.—**Jose Higueras**.

I don't care who you are, you're going to choke in certain
matches. You get to a point where your legs don't move
and you can't take a deep breath. I've done it. Sure I have. I
did it at the beginning of the fifth set against Ilie Nastase
in the 1972 Open. I could feel it happening. You'd start to
hit the ball about a yard wide, instead of inches.—**Arthur
Ashe**, former captain of the American Davis Cup team,
talking about pressure during the US Open.

1983
Ask Nureyev to stop dancing, ask Sinatra to stop singing,
then you can ask me to stop playing.—**Billie Jean King** at
Wimbledon.

These kids don't go to parties, they don't socialise.
Everybody is concerned about practising, playing tennis,
not talking to anybody. It's a business. Women's tennis has
become junior tennis as far as I'm concerned.—**Rosie
Casals** on the teenage 'phenoms'.

1984
New Yorkers love it when you spill your guts out there.
Spill your guts at Wimbledon and they make you stop and
clean it up.—**Jimmy Connors** at Flushing Meadow.

Shut your fat frog mouths.—**McEnroe** to President's box
in Paris.

This is unbelievable. I usually show up Monday, lose Tuesday and go home Wednesday.—**Vijay Amritraj** on reaching the Stockholm doubles final with Nastase.

I don't know that my behaviour has improved all that much with age. They just found somebody worse.—**Jimmy Connors**.

I'd bet my house she couldn't beat the 100th-ranked male player. And two houses she couldn't beat Harold Solomon.—**Vitas Gerulaitis** on Martina Navratilova.

Even the men over 40 could beat us. My brother still beats me, and he isn't ranked. Martina would lose to the top 1,000 men.—**Chris Evert-Lloyd**.

For two weeks I've been seeing the ball like a basket-ball. Today I couldn't find it.—**Jimmy Connors** after losing 6–1, 6–1, 6–2 to McEnroe at Wimbledon.

1985
Be patient. She's British.—**Chris Evert-Lloyd** on her new doubles partner, Jo Durie.

INDEX